Praise for *God Is My CEO*

"Many leaders, whether newly indoctrinated to the world of business or veteran executives, will find tools for the trade in this excellent guidebook."

—*Publishers Weekly*

"Newcomers to the business world will find nuggets of gold in these pages and the more seasoned traveler will find an oasis where they can be rejuvenated."

—Stan Geyer, President and CEO,
Flouroware

"*God Is My CEO* should be read by all CEOs or anyone in a leadership position. If your company is driven by mission rather than the bottom-line, this book will strengthen your position."

—Anne Beiler, Founder and CEO,
Auntie Anne's Hand-Rolled Soft Pretzels

"The practical approach of having CEOs give their answers to real-life situations is an extremely practical way to give advice. What's most important, however, is the biblical foundation which has been authenticated in the lives of the men and women highlighted in *God Is My CEO*."

—Wes Cantrell, Chairman and CEO,
Lanier Worldwide, Inc.

"In challenging times, those leaders who can reach deep within themselves and draw upon an inner strength fortified by strong moral values and a depth of character—those leaders will be successful. *God Is My CEO* provides the guide to those values and that depth of character. It is a must-read for those who lead the efforts of others."

—General Charles C. Krulak (Ret.),
31st Commandant, U.S. Marine Corps
Chairman and CEO, MBNA Europe

God
is my
CEO

*Following God's Principles
in a Bottom-Line World*

Larry S. Julian

Adams Media Corporation
Avon, Massachusetts

Published by
Adams Media Corporation
57 Littlefield Street, Avon, MA. USA.
www.adamsmedia.com

ISBN: 1-58062-477-4

Printed in Canada.

J I H G F E D

Library of Congress Cataloging-in-Publication Data

Julian, Larry S.
    God Is My CEO : following God's principles in a bottom-line
world / Larry S. Julian.
        p. cm.
    Includes index.
    ISBN 1-58062-477-4
        1. Businesspeople—Religious life. 2. Business—Religious
aspects—Christianity. I. Title: God is my chief executive officer.
II. Title.
BV4596.B8 J85 2001
248.8'8—dc21   00-050254

The *Life Application Study Bible: New International Edition* was used for biblical
references throughout this book. Published by Tyndale House Publishers, Wheaton,
IL, 1997.

This publication is designed to provide accurate and authoritative information with
regard to the subject matter covered. It is sold with the understanding that the publisher is not engaged in rendering legal, accounting, or other professional advice. If
legal advice or other expert assistance is required, the services of a competent professional person should be sought.
—From a *Declaration of Principles* jointly adopted by a Committee of the American
            Bar Association and a Committee of Publishers and Associations

Many of the designations used by manufacturers and sellers to distinguish their
products are claimed as trademarks. Where those designations appear in this book
and Adams Media was aware of a trademark claim, the designations have been
printed in initial capital letters.

This book is available at quantity discounts for bulk purchases.
For information, call 1-800-872-5627.

Dedication

To my Lord, Jesus Christ.
Thank you for the privilege of it all.

Contents

introduction

The Clash of Two Worlds / xv

chapter one

Purpose / 1

chapter ten

Priorities / 207

conclusion

A Message of Hope / 235

Acknowledgments

Dear Lord,

Almost six years ago, I wrote my first words dedicating this book to you. Thank you for somehow guiding me through a process completely foreign to me. I have now come to understand how You bless me through others.

To my wife, Sherri, who has blessed me beyond my imagination. Very simply, this book would not have been written without her. She is more than my wife, she is my hero. She defines what a wife of character is. My feelings are best summed up by Proverbs 31:29, "Many women do noble things, but you surpass them all."

To our two children in heaven, who taught me that life is a gift to be received and to be given away.

To our newborn daughter, Grace, who has brought to life the true meaning of God's grace.

To our families, who support us through their prayers and unconditional love: Ma, Dad, Lolly, Matt, Scott, Judy, Steve, and Lesley.

To my mentor and friend, Monty Sholund. Not only did you teach me, but you supported me, and encouraged me to pursue God with all my heart.

To Lamar Hamilton, for his desire to serve God and for being God's instrument in connecting me to the most important people in my life. To Ron James, who taught me to be at peace where I am. He always seemed to appear at a time I needed him. To Bill Hardman, who shined God's light to help me during my darkest moments. To Marc Belton, who gave me encouragement and support in every step of the book-writing process.

To Tanya Dean, who taught me how to write a story, then encouraged and guided me through the process of writing an entire book.

To Minneapolis business leaders Stan Geyer, Jay Bennett, Kenny Owen, Warren McLean, Frank Brantman, Rick Collins, Mike Sime, Jackie West, Jim Gabbert, and Larry Youngblood, who share my love for the Lord and showed their support for the book in so many ways.

To my fellow speakers Glenna Salsbury, David McNally, and Dick Schaaf, who showed me how to traverse the trials of authorship.

To my good friends Jim Walter, John Zapalla, and Marty Sinacore for 30 years of friendship. To my friends Dwight and Rhonda Schneibel, Doug and Melanie Peterson, and Steve and Barb Gretch, for their constant support and prayers for Sherri and me over the past three years. To my friends Kevin McArdle, Steve Waller, and Andy Anderson, who have supported me, past and present.

And last, but not least, to the 20 leaders who shared their stories. They gave not only their time, but they gave their hearts so they could be a blessing to us all.

The Clash of Two Worlds

Issue: We are led by bottom-line pressures.

For a man is a slave to whatever has mastered him.

−2 Peter 2:10

I was recently asked to conduct a leadership program for a group of San Francisco sales executives. As part of my preparation, the leader asked me to weave in a module on stress management. During the program, I discovered that the entire group was on the brink of a collective nervous breakdown. They were all under relentless pressure to produce results. All felt as if they were strapped to a treadmill whose speed kept increasing.

I wanted to help them find the root cause of their situation. The group, however, wanted me only to equip them with skills so that I could help them run their treadmill faster and better. In essence, they wanted me to teach them how to go down the wrong path more efficiently.

The bottom line had become their god. It was insatiable. No matter how hard they worked, it was never enough, nor would it ever be enough. These executives were talented, intelligent, capable people who, somewhere along the way, lost focus on what is truly meaningful and important. They had become slaves to bottom-line pressure and, as a result, became professionally ineffective and personally burnt out.

Solution: Let God lead.

Trust in the Lord with all your heart, and lean not on your own understanding. In all your ways acknowledge Him, and He shall make your paths straight.

—Proverbs 3:5–6

In my work as a management consultant, I find people in all positions, from CEOs to line employees, wrestling with challenging dilemmas and trying to make sense out of situations that have no simple solutions. These are talented people who want to make a difference, but who are stuck in a quagmire of urgent deadlines, unrealistic expectations, and politics.

There are times when critical business decisions have no correct answer and can only be made with a leap of faith by the leader alone. The solution is to trust God's principles, which will help us be effective and significant leaders in the midst of a pressured and demanding world.

A ship that turns its direction by one degree will alter its course by hundreds of miles. In the same way, your trust in God will have a significant impact on the direction you're headed. The more you trust, the more freedom you will gain from the shackles of the urgent, bottom-line pressures that enslave you. The more freedom you have, the more significant a leader you become.

Biblical Principles versus Bottom-Line Demands

At our very core, we want meaning and purpose in our work. We are looking for appreciation and affirmation for our contributions, satisfying answers to ethical dilemmas, clarity and direction in the midst of confusion, and a sense of fulfillment. This common theme crosses every layer of management and extends across races, nationalities, religions, and genders.

We usually want to do the right thing but often succumb to the short-term, bottom-line demands of daily business life. While we are encouraged to follow God on Sunday, we are not supported to make the right ethical decisions in the trenches on Monday through Friday.

This paradigm has demanded that we operate in two separate worlds: a deeply personal, private, spiritual world and a very public, demanding, competitive business world. For the most part, these two worlds clash in their values, beliefs, and principles, and we are caught in the middle.

This separation between a true longing for meaning in the workplace and the demand to help our employers survive and thrive creates a tremendous internal dilemma. The elements of this dilemma are shown on the following page.

Business Principles versus God's Principles

Unwritten Business Rules	God's Principles
• Achieve results	• Serve a purpose
• What can I get?	• How can I give?
• Success = dollars	• Significance = people
• Work to please people	• Work to please God
• Fear of the unknown	• Living with hope
• Leadership is being first	• Leadership is being last
• Take charge; surrender means defeat	• Let go; surrender means victory
• The end justifies the means. Get to the outcome regardless of how you accomplish it.	• The means justify the end. Do the right thing regardless of the outcome.
• Short-term gain	• Long-term legacy
• Slave to the urgent	• Freedom of choice
• You can never produce enough	• Unconditional love

We commonly view this dilemma as an internal struggle between right and wrong. We seem to be presented with a disturbing choice: either we embrace bottom-line success and turn from God, or we accept and live by God's principles and suffer whatever negative business consequences come our way. We are challenged by questions like "Can I do what's right and be successful in a competitive, bottom-line world?" and "Can I be both ethical and profitable?"

If you trust in God's principles, have the courage to live them, and have the patience to wait on His timing, then I believe the answer to these questions is "Yes." Biblical principles and bottom-line success are not opposites. Yes, *you can* do what's right and be successful. Yes, *you can* be both ethical and profitable. And yes, *you can* honor God, serve others, and fulfill your professional obligations.

God did not call us to be victims of circumstance. He calls us to grow closer to Him by courageously working through our dilemmas. He wants us to prosper, to be valuable leaders, and to serve as models to help others.

God's design of leadership has a solid foundation and center and is built to grow stronger over time *in the midst of external pressure.* This leadership model utilizes time and pressure to yield wisdom, growth in character, and maximum productivity.

When you integrate God's principles with your unique talents, skills, and character, you create a powerful partnership for being successful *in* the world without becoming *of* the world. As a result, your *challenges and dilemmas strengthen you* to become the successful and significant leader God intended you to be.

God's wisdom, your spiritual core, provides your source of strength, purpose, and direction and balances and leverages your skills and abilities. **Your character** is the aggregate sum of who you are as you courageously follow through and do what's right over time. **Your productivity** is the legacy you leave behind. Like diamonds, godly leaders brilliantly reflect God's nature in all circumstances and shine brightly in the toughest of times.

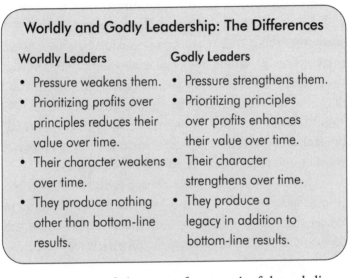

Worldly and Godly Leadership: The Differences

Worldly Leaders	Godly Leaders
• Pressure weakens them.	• Pressure strengthens them.
• Prioritizing profits over principles reduces their value over time.	• Prioritizing principles over profits enhances their value over time.
• Their character weakens over time.	• Their character strengthens over time.
• They produce nothing other than bottom-line results.	• They produce a legacy in addition to bottom-line results.

At the core of the quest for meaningful work lies a clash between two masters who demand to be first in your heart and mind. In the end, you have to choose.

Your future is determined by what you believe and do. Every one of your beliefs generates behavior, and every behavior has a consequence. Ultimately, *you become what you believe and do every day.* As Charles Reade stated, "Sow an act and you reap a habit; sow a habit and you reap a character; sow a character and you reap a destiny."

It is essential to understand the impact of your beliefs and actions, because they are shaping your future. What are the beliefs that drive your business decisions? Does your faith define who you are at work, or do the business rules define who you are? Are you on the right path?

The beauty and infinite wisdom of God provide us with the freedom to think and choose. This book is not about preaching religion, nor is it a debate about what is right or wrong. Rather, this book is about helping you make the right choices in challenging circumstances. Your dilemmas are natural stepping stones on your path to success. The goal of this book is not to provide you with prepackaged solutions to your dilemmas but to help you work through the process of solving them yourself.

Very simply, this book is intended to help you reflect on your beliefs and to seek God to equip and encourage you to do the right thing under pressure. This process will put you on the most important and meaningful path in your life.

How this book will help you

In order for you to become a successful godly leader, you should be regularly developing and integrating these two areas:

1. The outer development of your God-given talents and skills.

2. The inner development of your spiritual core. This development occurs as a result of wholehearted pursuit and practice of God's principles.

Thousands of leaders have great external leadership skills but no inner character. There are also many people of great character who do not have the necessary leadership skills. This book will help you combine these two elements to help you become a successful and significant leader.

Throughout this book, you will reflect upon and respond to what is most important in your life and business rather than react and do the things you are pressured to do. You can reflect on God's principles and use them as potential solutions to difficult and confusing business issues.

To accomplish this, you will need to rise above the superficial business pressures to gain a bigger perspective. We will explore the 10 most common issues facing business people today and apply God's principles to these dilemmas. You can make the right choices and become the successful and significant person God has intended you to be.

Each chapter will do three things for you:

1. Help you gain ideas and encouragement from the real-life stories of 20 leaders who have faced the same challenges.

2. Share God's principles as an alternative way to help you make wise decisions in the midst of challenging circumstances.

3. Provide a simple and practical Discussion Guide to help focus your thoughts and move you forward with a sense of purpose.

A final thought on your quest

This book is designed to help you make two important connections. First, it will help you connect with other leaders in a safe, nonthreatening way to share ideas and insights on being a godly leader. Second, and most important, it will help you reconnect with God in your workplace. As you move through this book, remember why you are taking on this effort. God loves you, has a purpose for your life, and wants you to succeed. As you focus on your spiritual growth, keep in mind that you are being prepared for significant rewards far beyond what you can possibly imagine. Enjoy the journey.

DISCUSSION GUIDE

1. Describe the risks and rewards of being a godly leader in a bottom-line world.

2. Review the chart listing the unwritten business rules and God's principles. What beliefs (from either side of the chart) currently drive your business decisions?

3. What erroneous belief enslaves you the most and hinders your effectiveness?

4. What specific steps can you take to eliminate or reduce this erroneous belief?

5. Which godly principle means the most to you and why?

6. What specific steps can you take to live by that principle?

Purpose

From earning a living to serving a purpose

*In all things God works for the good
of those who love Him, who have
been called according to His purpose.*

–Romans 8:28

Issue: How do I find meaning and purpose in my work?

I was helping an executive team clarify their mission statement. I began by asking the fundamental question, "What is the purpose of your company?" They never answered the question. Instead, they focused on developing words and phrases that would sound appealing to their shareholders, customers, and employees. They spent hours wordsmithing phrases such as "maximizing profitability," "world-class service," and "our employees are our greatest asset." Hours had been spent on the words, but there was no meaning behind them.

It was almost noon when the company's president arrived. He walked into the room, glancing at the white flipchart sheets with the carefully created phrases. Turning to the group, he said, "Let me bottom-line this. Our purpose is to increase revenue 15% and we have 11 months and 10 days to do it."

Employees look for meaning and purpose in their work, yet in reality the bottom-line pressure for company profitability often takes precedence over employee or company meaning and purpose. Is there more to work than earning a paycheck? The answer is yes, but we need to look in the mirror and honestly ask ourselves, "What is our priority? What purpose do we serve?" "And to what end?" Finding the answers to these questions will help us find our true calling.

Solution: Find God's calling and find your purpose.

God wants us to be successful. Not only does He plant the motivation in our hearts but He also gives us an intrinsic desire to contribute, add value, and connect with others in some meaningful endeavor. Finding meaning and purpose in our work is the key to both personal fulfillment and professional success.

Our purpose drives everything else: what we do, how we do it, and for whom we work. It gives us a reason to get out of bed every morning and gives direction to our days.

In this chapter, we will first learn how Bill George's journey led him to become CEO of Medtronic, providing him with personal fulfillment after a 30-year search. Then, we will learn from Bill Pollard, Chairman and CEO of The ServiceMaster Company, whose brand-names include TruGreen-Chemlawn, Merry Maids, and Terminix, among others, how creating meaning and purpose for employees is the key to his organization's success. In both cases, we will see how turning to God to find meaning and purpose can lead to both personal and professional fulfillment and success.

What is the key to their impressive track records in growth and profitability? In both companies, their mission, or purpose, takes precedence over profitability. Shareholder profits and long-term growth have been the result of their mission, not the mission itself.

3

BILL GEORGE
"Finding Your Way Home"

W hether in an entry-level position or as CEO, most people long to find meaning and purpose in their work. For Bill George, CEO of Medtronic, the world's largest therapeutic medical technology company and supplier of more than half the pacemakers implanted throughout the world, it was a 30-year journey through a maze of challenges, opportunities, and some disillusionment before he finally came to the place he could call home, a place to finally fulfill his calling and make a difference—God's way.

In San Francisco, Grace Cathedral on Nob Hill is a special place for Bill and his wife Penny. On the grounds, there is a beautiful labyrinth, an intricate maze that winds its way to the center. Trying to figure out the right path can be frustrating. There are roadblocks and choices between left and right turns before getting to the center. Bill sees the journey through the maze as a metaphor for the process of finding true meaning and purpose in his life.

One of those choices has been Bill's main conflict: trying to discern between God's calling for his life and his ego. "Since I was a teenager," says Bill, "I felt that God had a mission for my life. I felt that my mission was to become the head of a major corporation so I could influence other leaders by the way I conducted myself. Making a difference was a very important drive in my life. Sometimes I got confused on who I was making a difference for. Many times, making a difference translated into ego, recognition, and power. I had to constantly challenge myself by asking, 'For whom?' 'For what purpose?'"

Bill's quest to fulfill his calling was very much on track. However, the sense of fulfillment that comes from being aligned with God's calling was drifting away. From a business perspective, Bill was on a fast track toward becoming CEO of a major corporation. His resume included Harvard Business School and President of Litton Microwave. By 1983, he was one of the top five executives at Honeywell. As Bill rose to the top of Honeywell, he received many job offers from around the country. One of the pursuing companies was a small, Minneapolis-based company called Medtronic. Medtronic first approached Bill to become their President and CEO in 1978, again in 1986, and yet again in 1988.

Bill repeatedly turned down each offer because Medtronic didn't fit into his calling. His ego told him that a $750 million company wasn't enough to satisfy his ambitions because he was already running a $2 billion organization with three times the number of employees.

Though Bill knew of Medtronic's fine reputation, he turned down each offer as he single-mindedly moved toward his goal. He felt he was getting closer and closer to what he thought was his calling, but in reality, he was drifting further and further away. He explains, "I was trying to change the culture at Honeywell to reflect my values and philosophy. In reality, the culture at Honeywell was changing me. I realized that I was acting out a role designed to get ahead."

Bill was in charge of nine divisions, and eight of them were out of town. As time went on, he became more intense and felt more uptight, like he was on a treadmill. The harder he ran, the faster the treadmill sped up. But he wasn't going anywhere. It became clear to Bill that he was running so hard he couldn't stop long enough to hear God's voice.

For many years, Bill continued to pursue his goal to be CEO of a major corporation, believing that was the platform he needed to carry out God's call. In the fall of 1988, he finally hit the wall. One day, as he was driving home from work around Lake of the Isles, Bill looked around at the beauty of the community where he lived. The fall foliage was starting to come out in the grand maple-lined parkway that surrounded the lake. This beautiful picture reminded him of a very special retreat weekend he had participated in that was put on by the Episcopal church back in 1974.

"I realized back then that I had compartmentalized my life into work, home, spiritual, and community," Bill relates. "At that retreat, I knocked down the walls, making one big room. It gave me the freedom to be who I am. I realized that I let the world compartmentalize me back then, and now I was allowing it to happen to me again. When I saw the beauty of Lake of the Isles, it represented the open room. That vision made me stop and think, 'Here's this wonderful life I have been blessed with and I'm wandering in the desert. Where am I going?'"

Bill realized that his current job situation was changing him in ways he didn't like. "I might become CEO of Honeywell or I could wind up taking a job as CEO of some undefined company in some unknown community just to satisfy my ego's ambitions, all of which would force my wife, Penny, to quit her job and cause our sons to change schools just as they were coming into their high school years at a school they both loved. And why? To satisfy my ego to be CEO of a major corporation? To what end?"

That evening Bill talked to Penny about his new insights, and the two of them prayed together. He openly questioned if it was important to be CEO of a megacorporation. For the first time he saw clearly that such things were of little or no importance. Bill refocused on what was important: his marriage to Penny, their family, their friends, their ties to the community, and the opportunity to make a big difference in a smaller company with great potential.

Bill explains, "Nothing against Honeywell, but I needed a change in venue and a change in outlook. I needed time to listen, really listen to the inner voice that is the Lord's calling. I asked a close friend to call Win Wallin, then CEO of Medtronic, and tell him that I was available after all if the job was still open. I was fortunate to find that the position was still available."

Earl Bakken, the founder of Medtronic, met with Bill in Phoenix while he was on a business trip. Earl had taken the time to fly from Hawaii to meet with the potential new CEO. Talking with Earl, Bill had the sense that he had found the place where his calling could be realized. "It was an immediate values fit," Bill recalls. "This was meant to be. I was fortunate enough to get the job. The moment I stepped through the doors at Medtronic, I knew I had come home."

Now, 11 years later, Bill realizes that Medtronic was where he belonged all along. At Medtronic he can openly express and share his values, dreams, hopes, and fears. Through Medtronic's unique mission, written in 1960 by founder Earl Bakken, Bill can help carry out God's call to restore people to full life and health, and he can act as an ethical servant leader. "The 'call' had been there since 1978, yet I hadn't heard it. More precisely, I wasn't prepared to receive it. I had to go through the maze before I came to the center, which was God's call, not mine."

As a result, Bill and Penny's marriage is better than ever, and their sons, off on their own, are doing very well. Bill even went back to coaching soccer; this time he was more relaxed and caring than ever.

Bill's eyes light up when he talks about Medtronic's mission. "The previous companies I worked for had good values, but we couldn't discuss the things that were meaningful in our lives. At Medtronic, people talk about their faith and values all the time. Open discussion is encouraged because talking about values creates bonding to others and to a meaningful common purpose. The employees at Medtronic are committed to our mission of restoring people to full life and health."

Bill explains that Medtronic is successful because it is a mission-driven company. Medtronic is not in the business of maximizing shareholder value. They are in the business of maximizing the value of the patients they serve. "That's what motivates our people!" says Bill. "My entire work experience leads me to believe that people want to find genuine meaning in their work, to believe that they are working for a higher purpose, to believe that they can make a difference in the lives of others. At Medtronic, if we serve our patients well, we will do very well and increase our shareholder value a lot. If our 23,000 employees are motivated by the same common purpose, we will be very successful."

Medtronic's leaders work very hard to achieve an open dialogue with all employees. They do this through several vehicles: informal employee breakfasts; new employee sessions with the founder, Earl Bakken, or Bill; a holiday party; all-employee meetings; and a wide range of one-on-one sessions. For example, the company personally gives a special medallion that represents Medtronic's mission to every employee who joins the company. Bill explains, "We say to the employee, 'This medallion can only be given to a Medtronic employee. By accepting this medallion you are making a commitment to give your best effort to restoring people to full life and health.' This simple gesture is very meaningful to our employees. It tells them that their work has meaning—it goes beyond just earning a buck."

Bill finds that, almost without exception, his employees are motivated to achieve the unsurpassed quality called for in the Medtronic mission. They look for meaning in their work, a meaning that is usually underpinned by a solid spiritual base. The company has a wide of range belief systems represented: Christians, Jews, Muslims, Hindus, Buddhists, and many who have no established faith at all. But there is a sense that all are on a common path, searching for deeper meaning and fulfillment in their work, for the ability to help and serve others.

Medtronic celebrates its mission at the annual holiday party, a tradition for the past 40 years. Every year six people come in to share how the employees at Medtronic have made a difference in their lives. Even though Medtronic helped restore 2.5 million people back to full health and life in 1998, for example, it is more personalized when one person tells the employees, "If it weren't for you, my two-year-old daughter wouldn't be here today. You saved her life."

Just listening to Bill convinced me that Medtronic employees are truly motivated by serving a higher purpose. Although he was somewhat reserved at the beginning of our interview, when we started discussing the people at Medtronic, Bill exuded a powerful sense of passion and fulfillment. After a brief pause, I asked him, "What about you? How did you redefine your calling to find your fulfillment?"

Suddenly Bill jumped up and walked over to his desk. I was startled, thinking perhaps I had offended him and the interview was over. Then I noticed the huge grin on his face as he walked back to the table. Bill handed me a framed picture.

"This is T.J. When I first started at Medtronic, the company was faced with a division that was losing a lot of money. We were losing approximately five million dollars a year and had already lost about thirty-five to forty million dollars. We were ready to shut the division down. But then I met T.J. at my first holiday party." Bill explained that T.J. had cerebral palsy and had come to the holiday party to share what it meant to be functional, thanks to the drug pump that this "losing" division manufactured. T.J. became a real-life example of Medtronic's mission. Bill found it easy to relate to him because T.J. was the same age as Bill's son. T.J.'s story enlivened everyone. Bill says, "After the holiday party, we all got together with one goal in mind: How can we make this division work? We found a way to restructure the division and today it is one of our most profitable divisions." No doubt, Bill's passion for helping people has empowered his employees to meet such challenges.

One could argue that Bill has already fulfilled his calling. He is CEO of the world's preeminent medical technology company. Revenues have grown 23.7% to $4.13 billion. The market value of Medtronic has exploded from $3.6 billion to around $60 billion as earnings have grown at a 26% rate. All of this sounds impressive, but I had to research Medtronic's financial results for myself because Bill never mentioned them during our interview. Bill was too busy talking about T.J., particularly T.J.'s accomplishments since they had met in 1989. "I am so proud of T.J. He is now 24 years old and doing extremely well. He is married, has graduated from college, has a good job, and is leading a very successful life."

Finally, I asked Bill if he thought he had achieved his original mission now that he is the head of a major corporation. Bill responded, "I don't think I had the influence on CEOs the way I originally planned. However, I now feel like I am fulfilling my mission, as I am able to influence many more people, of all ages, than I ever dreamed possible and understand what it means to serve others through your business."

It was evident observing the joy on Bill's face as he talked about his family, Medtronic's employees, and T.J., that Bill had found his calling. It is the same joy we get when we come home.

C. WILLIAM POLLARD
"Serving a Higher Purpose and Making Money"

How does one honor God, allow employees to find meaning and purpose in their work, and run a profitable business? One could easily argue that the reason for being in business is to make money and that while finding meaning and purpose is a noble pursuit, maximizing shareholder profits is the priority. ServiceMaster, a nationwide service business, is very profitable, but to the 250,000 employees who serve more than five million customers in 30 countries, their work provides much more than just profits.

Imagine a shareholder walking through ServiceMaster's lobby at their Downers Grove, Illinois, headquarters and seeing a marble statue of Christ washing the feet of a disciple. Beyond the statue is a wall that stands 18 feet tall and stretches 90 feet across. Engraved in the wall are these four statements that constitute the company's objectives:

To honor God in all we do
To help people develop
To pursue excellence
To grow profitably

Clearly, these statements are unusual for a publicly held company. We could, in fact, say they are controversial. How does Bill Pollard, Chairman and CEO of ServiceMaster, explain to shareholders that ServiceMaster's mission to serve God takes a higher priority than profits?

In his insightful book, *The Soul of the Firm,* Bill Pollard describes how this question was posed at one of ServiceMaster's shareholder meetings. One shareholder, while praising ServiceMaster for its profit performance, made the following statement: "While I firmly support the right of an individual to his religious convictions and pursuits, I totally fail to appreciate the concept that ServiceMaster is, in fact, a vehicle for the work of God. The multiple references to this effect, in my opinion, do not belong in the annual business report. To interpret a service for profit (which is what ServiceMaster does) as the work of God is an incredible presumption. Furthermore, to make a profit is not a sin. I urge that next year's business report be confined to just that—business."[1]

Bill Pollard disagrees. Not only does he believe that God belongs in the business world, but he also believes that helping employees find meaning and purpose at work is the key to his organization's success. "God and business do mix," says Bill, "and profit is a standard for determining the effectiveness of our combined efforts. For us, the common link between God and profit is people. But we live and work in a diverse and pluralistic society, and some people may either question the existence of God or have different definitions for God. That is why at ServiceMaster we never allow religion or the lack thereof to become a basis for exclusion or how we treat each other professionally or personally. At the same time, I believe the work environment need not be emasculated to a neutrality of no belief."[2]

The leaders at ServiceMaster believe that God has given each one of the employees dignity, worth, potential, and freedom to choose. The goal is to build a firm that begins with God and accepts and develops the different people He created. In fact, it has been the key to ServiceMaster's success. This simple truth of recognizing the potential, dignity, and worth of the individual has been one of the most important factors in the success and growth of their business.

Bill George showed how saving lives adds meaning and purpose to each Medtronic employee's work. But how does an organization like ServiceMaster recognize and develop the potential, dignity, and worth of an employee who performs mundane tasks like mopping floors? Part of the answer is in leadership's role in providing dignity and respect.

Bill Pollard himself made a meaningful connection with ServiceMaster. A college administrator, professor, and lawyer, Bill was at a point in his life where change was imminent. He found himself faced with two very different career paths. He had an offer to become partner of a major law firm and an offer for a senior management position at ServiceMaster. The position at the law firm made more sense; it was a job he was comfortable doing and it offered a better financial package. The ServiceMaster opportunity was more of an unknown that would lead Bill into uncharted waters. However, Bill was intrigued by ServiceMaster's mission. He shared its values and saw an opportunity to pursue a meaningful mission and to learn more about himself and others. With a desire to learn the true meaning of service and servant leadership, Bill took a leap of faith and accepted the position at ServiceMaster.

He immediately understood and connected with employees' viewpoints. In one of ServiceMaster's programs, We Serve Day, every leader in the organization has the opportunity to participate in directly serving the customer. As part of Bill's training, he had to perform tasks that front-line service employees perform every day. He was assigned to work with the housekeeping team at Lutheran General Hospital. In particular, he would be cleaning corridors, patient rooms, and bathrooms. One special incident helped him understand the principles of dignity and worth and how these principles translate to employee meaning and purpose.

Bill, Chairman and CEO, was working in a busy corridor of a hospital. He was getting ready to mop the floor, and people were busy coming and going, back and forth. Suddenly a woman stopped and asked him, "Aren't you Bill Pollard?" He told her he was. The woman then introduced herself as a distant relative of his wife. She looked at Bill and his mop, then shook her head. "Aren't you a lawyer?"

she asked. Bill responded that he had a new job and noticed that some other people were gathering around. The woman seemed embarrassed and leaned toward Bill, whispering, "Is everything all right at home?"[3]

This incident gave Bill tremendous insight. ServiceMaster's mission came to life. Not only did he gain valuable insight into the work of ServiceMaster's employees, he was able to define what servant leadership is and how it defines the role of leadership at ServiceMaster.

Bill believes that at ServiceMaster leadership begins with their objectives: to honor God in all they do, to help people develop, to pursue excellence, and to grow profitably. He explains, "In John 13 we read the story of how Jesus took a towel and a basin of water and washed the disciples' feet. In so doing, He taught his disciples that no leader is greater than the people he leads, and that even the humblest of tasks is worthy of the leader to do. Thus our role and obligation as leaders involves more than what a person does on the job. We must also be involved in what that person is becoming and how the work environment is contributing to the process."[4]

The new mindset that sees people as primary sets ServiceMaster apart. ServiceMaster is not a manufacturing company; it is a service organization, employing people who serve. Bill feels that how well employees serve depends on how they are motivated, respected, and trained. "It is not just what we are doing, but what we are becoming in the process that gives us our distinct value and is uniquely

human," he explains. "Every firm should be able to articu-
late a mission that reaches beyond the task and provides a
hope that the efforts and activities of its people are adding
up to something significant—so significant, in fact, that
even more can be accomplished than is expected."[5]

Servant leadership is an important component in
helping an employee find meaning and purpose at work,
but how does the employee make that meaningful connection? Put bluntly, how does an employee find meaning and
purpose in cleaning a toilet?

Bill answered the question by telling about Shirley.
Shirley is a housekeeper in a 250-bed community hospital.
That isn't what makes her different. She's different from
other housekeepers because, after 15 years, she's still
excited about her work. Shirley has seen some changes.
She has been moved from floor to floor. The chemicals,
mop, and housekeeper's cart have been improved so she
actually cleans more rooms today than she did five years
ago. But some things never change. The bathrooms and toi-
lets are still germ-ridden; the dirt on floors has to be
mopped up; patients still spill things; and some doctors still
treat "the help" like lepers. But Shirley keeps humming
away. Why?

It all comes down to ServiceMaster's view of the work
they do. Bill explains, "When Shirley sees her task as
extending service to the patient in the bed and herself as an
integral part of supporting the work of the doctors and
nurses, she has a cause—a cause that involves the health

and welfare of others. She came to us, no doubt, merely looking for a job, but she brought to us an unlocked potential and desire to accomplish something significant. She recently confirmed the importance of her cause when she told me, 'If we don't clean with a quality effort, we can't keep the doctors and nurses in business; we can't accommodate patients. This place would be *closed* if we didn't have housekeeping.'"[6]

Shirley's story helps clarify how every employee, no matter how mundane his or her task, can find meaning in it, can contribute value to his or her organization, and can serve a higher purpose, besides earning a paycheck.

But how does ServiceMaster's commitment to helping employees find meaning and purpose translate into profitability? Bill tells us that their goal is to train, to equip, and to motivate people to be more effective at work. He believes that if a person has clear direction and a real reason to serve, then that employee is more dependable and responsive to meet, solve, and exceed customers' expectations.

"Where do you begin when you are faced with starting a $24.4 million contract in a large city school system?" Bill asks as an example. "Morale is low. More than 14,000 windows are broken in 161 schools. Racial tensions, insecurity among union leaders, and a high rate of absenteeism complicate your task. You have promised a turnaround. The school board members have their necks on the line for hiring an outside contractor, and they want results yesterday!"[7] His answer shouldn't surprise us.

"You begin with people. At the first meeting we had with the employees, we provided light refreshments. Everyone came to the meeting and listened to our presentation, but nobody took the food. After the meeting, we discovered why: They didn't realize the food was for them. They had never been asked to participate in a meeting where food or service was provided for them."[8]

That was just the beginning. The leaders of ServiceMaster cared for their workers and treated them with dignity and respect. Before long the same workers who had felt so badly about their jobs began to respond with enthusiasm. Three months later, all of the broken windows had been repaired, the air conditioning (which some teachers didn't even know existed) was working again, and the entire look of the grounds changed from unkempt pastures of weeds to well trimmed yards with attractive flowers.

When the contract's anniversary date came, it was time to assess and recognize the progress. The city's newspaper ran a front-page story that lauded the improvements. School principals stated that ServiceMaster had helped improve communications within schools and had paved the way to organizing the custodial, maintenance, and grounds departments so they could be more responsive to the needs of school personnel. ServiceMaster went beyond the customer's expectations while saving the school district more than $3 million. Most surprising of all, ServiceMaster did it with *the same people who had been there before.* What happened? Bill explains, "The difference began with the way we treated them as people. They already had the dignity and potential. All we needed to do was to unlock that potential and provide training, direction, and recognition. It all goes back to our objectives and how we view people."[9]

ServiceMaster proves that the intangibles of respect, dignity, and service can contribute to the tangibles of profits and growth. In a world with constant change, economic slumps, and revolving management theories, ServiceMaster has demonstrated stellar growth and profitability with 20 years of record growth.

As Bill Pollard clarifies, "The objectives of our firm are not just carved in stone on the lobby wall. You can see them working every day in the lives of our people."[10] ServiceMaster demonstrates that providing meaning and purpose to employees not only honors God, it is good business.

CONCLUSION

The common theme acknowledged by both Bill George and Bill Pollard is that finding meaning and purpose at work is a journey. Bill George described the journey as similar to going through a maze. You can't see the final destination; it's a matter of moving forward, trusting that God is leading you according to his purpose.

God never promised a straight path to success. Most likely, it is a maze filled with obstacles of all kinds. The question for each of us is whether we allow the obstacles to deter us or whether we move forward in spite of them. To move in the direction of the sun, a plant will go around obstacles until it blooms into a spectacular flower. The plant's purpose is to reach toward the sun. Like the flower, a clear understanding of our purpose will enable us to move around, jump over, or break through our obstacles and bloom in our work settings.

God *is* leading us. The knowledge that we live our life with God's help provides the confidence, conviction, and focus that will move us forward regardless of circumstances. We can begin to understand that we have been called to meaningful work that far transcends any present job description. God did not call us to work the majority of our lives just to survive, earning a paycheck and existing from weekend to weekend. God created each person for specific reasons, tasks, and purposes, and He equipped each one of us with the perfect combination of talents, skills, and abilities required to find fulfillment for our lives.

Jesus provided a fundamental principle to help us find meaning and purpose in our work. While a key to business success, it is possibly the most misunderstood and misinterpreted principle in business today. Teaching about money, Jesus stated, "No one can serve two masters. Either he will hate the one and love the other or he will be devoted to the one and despise the other. You cannot serve both God and money." His underlying principle was about priorities. Our priority determines our course and measures our progress.

Jesus never said that money or financial success was wrong. He did say that prioritizing money over God is wrong. There is a greater purpose in our work beyond just making money, whether for ourselves or our corporations.

The organization whose purpose was to grow by 15% let its desire for profits diminish the primary purpose of its business. As business decisions subtly communicate to customers and employees that profit is more valuable than customer satisfaction and employee worth, the business will ultimately suffer the consequences of its priorities.

Those of us who are leaders of an organization should work to create a mission in which our organization's purpose is more than just making money. We can trust that serving a higher purpose will lead to business success. As we learned from ServiceMaster, creating an environment that provides dignity and respect and allowing employees to find meaning and purpose in their work will cause those employees to bloom gloriously. As we saw with Medtronic, the more we communicate the mission in terms the employee can relate to (such as Medtronic's holiday parties), the more motivated the employee is. In both case studies, all stakeholders, including company shareholders, customers, and employees, understood the higher priority and purpose of the organization.

We can't minimize the struggle we may have in finding meaning and purpose in our work. Here are three suggestions to help us.

1. Find a home.

It's important to find the environment that unleashes your talents and recognizes your contributions. The environment that is right for one person may not be right for another. Both Bill Pollard and Bill George found the right organization in which to bloom. We are also being called to bloom—not only for our benefit, but for the benefit of others. This may mean leaving the safety of a present job and traveling into uncharted waters. It may mean staying where we are and blooming where we are already planted. Either way, it's important to connect with the environment that brings out the best in each of us.

2. Align work with passion.

Every job has its share of mundane tasks. Those tasks don't have to put out the flame that burns inside of us. It is our own responsibility to fan into flame the gift God has placed inside us. We can't settle for the comfort zone and security of a job that we are not passionate about. Like Bill Pollard, we must take a leap of faith to pursue our passion.

3. Trust that God has called you to work for a purpose.

We all struggle to find the right balance between earning a living and serving a purpose. This tension is both normal and necessary because it helps shape our journey. However, don't let the obstacles stop your journey. When you find yourself caught between two masters, choose God because He wants you to succeed. As Romans 8:31 reminds us, "If God is for us, who can be against us?"

DISCUSSION GUIDE

Part 1: Individuals looking for meaning and purpose at work

1. What do you love doing? What are you most passionate about?
2. What is your greatest satisfaction at work?
3. Are you in an environment that fully utilizes your talents and skills?
4. What would you do if you knew you couldn't fail?
5. Create your ideal job.

Part 2: Organizations who want to discover the true purpose of their business

1. Other than making money, why do you exist? What purpose do you serve?
2. How does your organization add value and contribute to the community, customers, and employees?
3. How does your work environment help employees find meaning and purpose in their work?
4. How will fulfilling your organization's mission make your organization competitive and profitable?

Notes

1. C. William Pollard, *The Soul of the Firm* (Downers Grove, IL: The ServiceMaster Foundation, HarperBusiness, Zondervan Publishing, 1996), 19–20.
2. Ibid, 20–21.
3. Ibid, 14–15.
4. Ibid, 130.
5. Ibid, 46.
6. Ibid, 46–47.
7. Ibid, 57.
8. Ibid, 57.
9. Ibid, 58.
10. Ibid, 23.

2

Success

From success to significance

*For I know the plans I have for you,
declares the Lord, plans to prosper you and not
harm you, plans to give you hope and a future.*

—Jeremiah 29:11

Issue: How do I define success?

The owner of the 75-employee manufacturing company was ready to turn management of the family business over to his son. Three of us sat at a table in Mark's office, when suddenly, the dad slammed the business plan on the floor and lashed out at his son, Mark. "You're an idiot! I can't believe what a loser of a son I have! I didn't build this business to have you destroy it!" Mark sat quietly in his chair, expressionless. He walked out of the office, disgusted. I was stunned. I searched for something to say that would comfort Mark. After an awkward pause, Mark said, "It's nothing new. He's been like that his whole life."

I followed Mark's dad out of the room. I looked him in the eye and asked, "Do you love your son?" He paused for a moment, then answered, "Of course I love my son. It's just that I spent 35 years busting my butt to give him a better life. I don't want him to throw it all away." Then he added, "I worked hard to be a success, and I don't want to lose that."

Mark's father defined success by working long hours and making a lot of money. While he loved his son, his pursuit of success had cost him dearly. He had become a financial success and a personal failure: a 70-year-old man with plenty of money but nothing to show for it. As a father, he left money, but no legacy. He left only pain and an emotionally abused son.

Solution: Expand your definition from making money to making a difference.

When I was working with Mark and his father, I read a wonderful book, *Halftime: Changing Your Game Plan from Success to Significance*, by Bob Buford. The book provides tremendous insight into how we define success. Bob likens a business career to a football game. In the first half of our life, we pursue success. We work hard, sacrifice, and expend energy to become financially successful. In the second half, we focus on significance, giving our experience, time, talent, and energy toward making a difference in people's lives and leaving a legacy. Bob Buford's book crystallizes how important it is for us to take a hard look at how we define success.

The next two stories describe how two leaders came to redefine their success and as a result lead lives of significance. Bob Buford, Founder of Leadership Network, shows us how precious time is and that *now* is the time to live a life of significance. Jerry Colangelo, owner of the Phoenix Suns Basketball Club and the Arizona Diamondbacks Baseball Club, provides an example of a business and community leader who has learned that success is fleeting but significance can last a lifetime.

Bob Buford

"From Success to Significance"

Bob Buford understands the appeal of pursuing financial success. As the president of a successful cable television company, the Leadership Network, he loved the excitement of business. He was also successful in his personal life; he had a loving relationship with his wife, Linda, and son, Ross. As Bob approached middle age, however, his thoughts started to focus on the next part of his life. He pondered a deep question as he entered the second half of his life: "What is most important in life?" Little did he know that the answer to that question was a phone call away.

Bob wrote his book from the lessons he learned during a very difficult time. One of the most powerful chapters, "Adios Ross," tells about the tragic loss of Bob's one and only child, Ross.

On the evening of January 3, 1987, Bob got a call from his brother Jeff. Jeff, obviously upset, told Bob that Ross and two of his friends had tried to swim across the Rio Grande, a wide and unpredictable river that separates southern Texas from Mexico. His next words would change Bob's world forever.

"Ross is missing in the Rio Grande,"[1] Jeff said, his voice heavy from the weight of such news. Over the next long moments, Bob discovered that 24-year-old Ross had decided to join two other young men to try to capture the experience of what it was like for illegal aliens when they cross the dangerous watery border into the United States, the land of opportunity. Ross had no thought that this could be the last adventure of his earthly life.

Jeff told Bob that the third young man had survived and was frantic about finding his two friends. Bob arrived at the Texas–Mexico border, the Rio Grande Valley, before daybreak the next day to join the search, which was already well underway and coordinated by the Texas Rangers. Airplanes, helicopters, boats, trackers with dogs—Bob hired anyone and anything that could help the rescue effort. But several hours later, with no sign of either young man to give him hope, Bob faced the fact that he would never again see Ross in this life.

After all efforts had been exhausted, Bob returned home. The search continued, but it would be spring, four months later, before Ross's body was found, 10 miles downriver. Earlier, during the cold winter months as Bob lived in an odd world between having and not having his son, the family found a handwritten copy of Ross's will on his desk at his Denver home. Dated February 20, 1986, it had been written less than a year before the fatal accident. But Ross's words warmed his father over that winter:

> Well, if you are reading my will, then, obviously, I'm dead. I wonder how I died? Probably suddenly, because otherwise I would have taken the time to rewrite this. Even if I am dead, I think one thing should be remembered, and that is that I had a great time along the way. More importantly, it should be noted that I am in a better place now.[2]

Ross's will ended with these words:

> In closing, I loved you all and thank you. You've made it a great life. Make sure you all go up instead of down, and I'll be waiting for you at heaven's gate. Just look for the guy in the old khakis, Stetson, and faded shirt, wearing a pair of Ray-Bans and a Jack Nicholson smile. I also thank God for giving me a chance to write this before I departed. Thanks. Adios, Ross.[3]

More than ever before, Bob realized how much he lived in two worlds. The first is the crazy business world of meetings, phone calls, deadlines, deals, profits, and losses. Bob explains, "That world is like a cloud; it's going to perish. The other world I live in is where Ross is now—the world of the eternal. And it's the reality of that latter world that allows me to respond, with confidence: Adios, Ross, *for now.*"[4]

It is this eternal perspective that makes Bob passionate for life and deeply aware of the responsibility to make the most of each day. Bob especially likes George Bernard Shaw's quote, "I rejoice in life for its own sake. Life is no brief candle to me. It's a sort of splendid torch which I've got hold of for the moment, and I want to make it burn as brightly as possible before handing it on to future generations."[5]

Ross lived each day of his life like that, with enthusiasm, passion, and joy, the one reason Bob considers his son a hero. Each day was fully used, not squandered in any way. Bob tells people, "[Ross] didn't shortchange himself, even though his days among us were so few. Ross's death, while tragic, was an inspiration to me to burn brightly while it is day."[6]

In spite of this tragedy, or perhaps because of it, Bob maintains a positive, passionate attitude. Most people are never the same after the tragic loss of a child. The incidence of subsequent divorce is high. Many people question the presence of God, and some reject God altogether. Few are able to deal with the loss in such a profound and significant way and to touch others deeply. But Bob has.

When I interviewed Bob, I wanted to talk with him about Ross, but I was apprehensive to ask such personally sensitive questions. I expected to meet a distinguished man with a reserved demeanor. I found a man full of passion.

Bob explained, "After Ross's death, my wife came to me and said, 'Let's sell the house,' which was her way of saying that material things meant less to her. It gave me the perspective that material things are not that important. For me, it gave me a sense of the whole of life, not just this part of life. There is a lot more to life than this brief period we are in. You either believe it or you don't, and I really, really believe it.

"There are two ways of processing events in life. One is reason and one is faith. Let's say our life is 3 feet long. Most of life is reasonable up to a point. We can use our reason for 2 feet and 11 inches. However, that last inch is incomprehensible. It makes no sense. We can't process bad things like the Holocaust, personal tragedy, or Ross's death. We go as far as reason will take us, but the spark of faith has to bridge the gap."

Bob is clearly living a life of significance. In the second half of his life, he turned over the day-to-day operations of his business to others and became the founder of Leadership Network (*www.leadnet.org*), a support service to leaders of large churches. The foundation has had significant impact, helping thousands of church leaders become more effective leaders. Bob has established a second organization to inspire, train, and provide examples of the success to significance movement that now embraces thousands of business and professional people called FaithWorks (*www.faithworks.net*). His book has sold more than 100,000 copies, and Bob is a sought-after speaker. More important, he is passionately following the life God has called him to pursue.

As I spoke to Bob, I couldn't help but contrast his life with that of Mark's dad. Bob had physically lost his son, yet Bob was alive relationally and spiritually. He was living his life to the fullest and making a significant impact on this earth. He was squeezing everything out of the life of the present and was excited about someday seeing Ross again in eternity. Mark's dad, on the other hand, had his son physically close to him, yet father and son tragically live lives of relational emptiness.

I asked Bob what advice he would give Mark's dad, a man who is miserable because he is retired, is in good health, but doesn't know what to do with the rest of his life, and for Mark, a young man who has mentally decided to coast through the rest of his career.

Bob responded, "I believe God has planted spiritual DNA in every human being. He has a destiny laid out for each and every one of us. We can choose to accept that destiny or not." He also believes that it is absolutely critical that people don't ever let their brains coast. "Don't mentally retire on the job and put your plane on autopilot. Work will become increasingly sterile and meaningless. Everyone will know that you have done that. You will become more cautious and become increasingly worried that younger people are out-competing you. You become risk-averse. It's not good for you and not good for your organization."

Bob continued, "Secondly, don't physically retire. The idea of retiring to full-time leisure is a very dangerous idea. I have seen too many cases where people spend more time on toys and less time on relationships. I have seen too many people wind up in divorce."

Instead of taking such a passive role, Bob suggests people consider finding a parallel career, one that addresses two questions: What am I good at, or what have I achieved? What am I passionate about? The foundation of this advice is Bob's belief that God calls and equips everyone with talents to pursue his or her unique calling. But it is up to each person to find a place to use those gifts and to fulfill a God-given destiny. This may not even involve much change. Bob suggests that we take our gifts and talents into account and fit them into what means the most to us: family, business, or volunteering, either part or full time. Says Bob, "The most important thing is to embark! Get going!"

Bob also believes in something he calls the Law of Unintended Consequences. He explains, "People discover in business that you embark with a plan, and even though things often turn out very differently than you planned, they do have a way of turning out. If you never embark, they will never turn out. For example, experts in the stock market will tell you that the market moves up big on 12 days a year, but the timing is utterly unpredictable. You have to be in the market in order to capitalize on the upturn. If you are on the sidelines waiting to time your move perfectly, it will never happen. People pursue their calling in the same way. They say, 'I will stay in my job now, and someday I will pursue my dreams.'"

Bob understands how difficult it is for people to pursue their dreams, but he believes strongly that it's sometimes as simple as taking a leap of faith. "I choose to believe that it is God who speaks quietly within us," Bob says, "that it is He who put the question deep within. And when we discover the answers, he reveals the meaning He has chosen for us to enjoy; He unveils the goal he has been keeping for us all along. I love how Paul puts it in Ephesians 2: 'For we are God's workmanship, created in Christ Jesus to do good works, which God prepared in advance for us to do.'"

Bob also commented that people like Mark and Mark's dad should have hope and see the latter half of their lives in a new light. He cited some trends that reaffirm how the second half of our lives can be filled with significance. Two major environmental and cultural shifts affect every individual in the latter half of his or her career: longevity and affluence.

"People are now living active lives into their 80s and beyond," Bob states. "People have a whole second adulthood that their grandparents never had. In many cases we have an extra 20 to 30 years of active adulthood remaining. What are we going to do with these extra 20 to 30 years? Overall, we are much more affluent than we were before. Many people don't need to work in order to live and survive. Most people spend a tremendous amount of time, energy, and resources toward their business but rarely do we apply the same time, energy, and resources toward the second half of our lives."

But Bob is a realist. He knows that, though few people want to put their careers ahead of their families, it happens. People want to be successful, and the pull is hard to resist. Choosing how we want to live is no less important for the second half of our lives than it is for the first. In fact Bob tells people, "You have the freedom to decide whether you want the rest of your years to be the best of your years."[7]

Bob Buford leads a significant life encouraging thousands of people like Mark, you, and me to make a difference during this brief time we have on this earth. He understands the pursuit of success, and he understands the pursuit of significance. He invites each of us to ponder the question, "How can I make the rest of my life the best of my life?"

JERRY COLANGELO
"From Me to We"

Jerry Colangelo is a leader who has redefined the word *success*. In business terms he's a success, the multimillionaire owner of two successful sports franchises, the Phoenix Suns Basketball Club and the Arizona Diamondbacks Baseball Club. More important than success to Jerry, however, is leading a life of significance.

"Success, unfortunately, is measured by how well one has done financially," explains Jerry. "Success, in my mind, is having your priorities right and being able to make a difference in other people's lives. For me, my priorities are God, family, and making a difference in the community." Jerry's shift from success to significance has been a long journey. Along the way, he turned to God, which helped him shift the focus of success from *me* to *we*.

Jerry Colangelo had dreams of being a big success in sports. In high school, he was a star in both baseball and basketball. In 1957, his senior year, he made the Illinois All-State High School Basketball Team. He received 66 scholarship offers from all around the country and received 6 offers from major league baseball franchises. At the age of 18, Jerry had a bright future ahead of him. He chose to attend the University of Kansas because they had the best basketball player in the country, Wilt Chamberlain, and the best chance to win the NCAA Championship.

Life, however, did not cooperate with Jerry's dreams. During his college years, things did not go as he planned. Wilt Chamberlain left Kansas to play for the Harlem Globetrotters. His dreams of winning a NCAA Championship dashed, Jerry returned home to attend Illinois State. Unfortunately, NCAA rules kept him from playing basketball for a year. To support his family, he worked for the City of Chicago Heights in the sewage department. It was a humbling experience for a well known athlete. Although an excellent basketball and baseball player throughout college, upon graduation, he was left with shattered dreams. Due to injuries, he had to quit baseball, and in basketball, he was never chosen in the NBA draft. His career in sports was over.

With his dream of being a successful athlete now shattered, Jerry turned to the business world. He went into the tuxedo rental business with an old friend in Chicago Heights. For three years, Jerry poured everything into the business. He worked long hours, plowing whatever profits were made back into the business, all to no avail. His business venture was a failure. At 26 years old, he found himself out of work with no future plans, struggling to support his wife, Joan, and their three young children.

Jerry was ready to redefine what success meant to him. He recalls, "Prior to this experience, it was all me, myself and I. I considered myself pretty capable of taking care of things. Whatever life threw at me, I could handle. I was so busy doing my thing, trying to build my business, that I didn't have a good picture of where I really needed to be in my life."

Jerry's wife Joan had been attending a small Baptist church, and Jerry started going with her. Because of Joan, Jerry began to understand and depend on his faith in God. He found that when a person humbles himself before God, things change: priorities, attitudes, and relationships. "I finally realized that I couldn't do it myself," Jerry explains. "I didn't know where I was going to be the next day, because I had nowhere to go, no place to turn."

In his book, *How You Play the Game,* Jerry describes an extraordinary occurrence that took place next. One day Jerry sat down at the kitchen table and, having nothing to do and nowhere to go, out of boredom Jerry took his wallet from his pocket and started cleaning it out. As he was tossing away random scraps of paper, he found a business card, crumpled and worn. Jerry guessed he'd been carrying it around for about two years. He remembered his father-in-law handing it to him one day, mentioning that Jerry should meet this man.

But Jerry had become busy with business and a growing family. So he forgot about the business card. As he looked down at the all-but-forgotten piece of paper, Jerry figured, "Why not?" He had lots of spare time and nothing to lose. In fact Jerry was at the bottom of his game—26 years old, making only $50 a game playing in a semiprofessional basketball league at night. The next morning Jerry called the man, Dick Klein. Dick invited Jerry to come to his office for an informal chat. Jerry agreed.

As it turned out, Dick Klein owned an incentive mer-
chandising company that assisted companies in putting
together gift packages and other programs to give to clients,
distributors, and suppliers. Dick ran a one-person shop and
was swamped with work. He hired Jerry to help in the business, but Jerry soon found that Dick's real passion was to
start a National Basketball Association (NBA) franchise in
Chicago. Jerry immersed himself in the incentive business
and, at the same time, had the opportunity to be a part of
Dick's dream of having a professional basketball team. Jerry
soon found himself learning everything about the business
side of sports from the ground up. As a result of calling
Dick Klein, Jerry Colangelo capitalized on the privilege and
opportunity of birthing the Chicago Bulls, one of the most
successful sports franchises in basketball.

During the Bulls' second year, the NBA expanded,
adding franchises in Seattle and San Diego. The following
year, the NBA expanded to Milwaukee and Phoenix. Jerry
was in demand, and he was looking for an opportunity to
become a General Manager. He received an offer to
become General Manager for the new Phoenix basketball
franchise for a salary of $22,500 per year. Jerry and his
family moved to Phoenix in 1968.

Finally, Jerry's faith and business came together. "Joan
and I had had an opportunity to chaperone a group of
teenagers for a Christian youth organization called Young
Life," says Jerry. "It made a big impression on me because
it helped me see what was important to young people.

When we moved to Phoenix a year and a half later, I mentioned this experience in the newspaper. Many families from the Young Life organization welcomed us to the Phoenix community. Being a part of the community meant a great deal to us."

Not only did Jerry recognize the importance of community from a personal viewpoint, he also recognized its value from a professional standpoint. The NBA was a relatively unknown commodity in Phoenix. He knew that success would start with a win-win relationship with the community. "From the start, my attitude was, 'This city doesn't owe us anything. The people of Phoenix do not owe us anything. We have to earn their support.'"[8]

From his start as General Manager to his eventual ownership of the Phoenix Suns and Arizona Diamondbacks, Jerry worked toward building a positive relationship with the community. He credits his faith and his commitment to integrity as the cornerstones to building a long-term relationship with the community. Jerry recalled, "The greatest thing you can say about a person is that he has integrity. I started with nothing financially. I got a 'character loan' to get me up and running. A character loan is what you receive when you have no capital."

Jerry credits his faith as the single most important factor in his success. "Life is not easy; it's a challenge," Jerry explains. "Successful people are those who can deal with challenges successfully. The truth is, the more public you are, the more opportunity you will have to fail, and fail in the most public and sometimes most embarrassing manner. You're dealing with the media, you're dealing with corporations, you're dealing with big business and high finance. In that potentially volatile mix, it's inevitable that you will make mistakes; a trade doesn't work out, a player doesn't live up to expectations, the arena needs more seats, the parking lot is too small, and so on."[9]

Jerry recalled one of the most painful experiences of his career. In 1986, a drug scandal hit the Phoenix Suns. Three players and two former players were arrested on drug charges. Although the charges never amounted to anything criminal and the case never went to trial, Jerry's reputation was dragged through the mud.

Phoenix was deluged by the media and reporters were like hounds on the hunt. It was clear to most people that they wanted someone's head. Jerry was the one they went after. They did their best to bring into question Jerry's character and reputation, and it looked as if all the work the organization had put into the community was going to go down the drain. Unable or unwilling to separate the man from the franchise, the media attacks made Jerry an object of ridicule. He was booed at games. It made no sense to him. Eventually, as is typical, the incident blew over and went away. But how did Jerry survive the storm? He explains, "Looking back, I couldn't see myself dealing with all of this without my faith."

Jerry Colangelo's 32-year partnership with the Phoenix community is not a story about winning or financial success;

it's a story about significance. "Over the years, I learned that things happen for a reason," says Jerry. "I once thought that success was being in the right place at the right time. I came to understand that it is God's plan, not mine. What pulls at my heart is to meet the needs of our community. God has given me a platform to bring together businesses, municipalities, social organizations, and charitable organizations to address all the needs of the community. My position gives me an opportunity to have more of an impact. I want to do as much as I can within reason to make as much impact as I can."

Recently, an old foe, the media, became a friend, providing testimony of Jerry Colangelo's life of significance. The *Arizona Republic* voted him Arizona's most influential sports figure of the century. The article read, "For changing the very scope of the community in which we live, Colangelo overwhelmingly was selected as Arizona's most influential sports figure of the century by the *Arizona Republic*'s sports staff. If this had been a horse race, Colangelo would have been Secretariat."[10]

CONCLUSION

How we define success is important in shaping our lives. So, how should we define success? Success is generally defined in terms of achievement, fame, recognition, material possessions, and wealth. In a word: *outcome*. Significance, on the other hand, while less tangible, concerns the *process*. Significance is importance, meaning, essence, relevance, and value. Success drives us by a desire for tangible things; significance guides us by a desire for something greater than just what is tangible.

Three common characteristics led Bob Buford and Jerry Colangelo on their paths to significance.

1. A Sense of Urgency

Bob and Jerry both have a sense of urgency. Because this life is short, the preciousness of life continually challenges them to prioritize what is most important. Both men live lives of daily significance, doing what they feel is most important every day. This sense of urgency translates into a passion for the moment. You can sense their aliveness.

Psalm 39:5 reminds us, "Each man's life is but a breath." If we are looking to lead lives of significance, we need to make it a priority *today*. Regardless of our age, it is not too late. Bob Buford offers the challenge: "The most important thing is to pull the trigger. Embark! Get going!"

2. A Sense of the Whole of Life

Both leaders have a sense of the whole of life, rather than just the part of life we can see today.

Bob Buford commented that Ross's death gave him a sense of the whole of life rather than this part of life. This core belief gave him an eternal perspective that helped him transcend the pain of his immediate tragic loss. He could have focused on the pain, but he chose to live the remainder of his life being significant in the present, while maintaining the hope of seeing his son again in the future. Jerry Colangelo learned to put wins and losses in their proper perspective. As a result, no obstacle or loss could prevent him from helping his community.

When we feel stuck or slowed down by pain, obstacles, or circumstances, we can remember that God has a bigger plan than what we are seeing in front of us. We can take a step back and sense the bigger picture and the whole of life. Then we can see our situation from a different perspective.

3. A Sense of Significance

Bob and Jerry both have a sense of significance. Rather than being driven by ego, they are driven by a calling. They believe they are here to make a difference in other people's lives. Everything they do is for something that is beyond just a tangible result. Bob has a passion to unleash the potential energy lying dormant in churches

today. Jerry's passion is to help meet needs in all
aspects of the Phoenix community. They each
have a passion to leave a legacy that affects thousands of others.

While we may not all be asked to change the
world, we can each affect one person in a meaningful way. What if Mark's dad had focused just
on building a relationship with him? What kind of
impact would that have had? Others need us. We
can make a big difference in their lives right now.
And that alone makes our lives significant.

DISCUSSION GUIDE

1. How do you define success?
2. How do you define significance?
3. If you had only one more year to live, what would you
   do with your year?
4. What are the obstacles that keep you from doing what
   you are passionate about?
5. If you were to make a shift from success to significance, what would it look like?
6. What legacy do you want to leave others?
7. What small thing can you do today that would make a
   difference in another's life?

Notes

1. Robert P. Buford, *Halftime* (Grand Rapids, MI: Zondervan Publishing, 1994), 55.
2. Ibid, 55–57.
3. Ibid, 57.
4. Ibid, 59.
5. Ibid, 59.
6. Ibid, 59.
7. Ibid, 166.
8. Jerry Colangelo with Len Sherman, *How You Play the Game* (New York: American Management Association, 1999), 61.
9. Ibid, 62.
10. "Colangelo pushed Valley teams' buttons," *Arizona Republic*, (December 26, 1999): Section C, Pages 1 and 8.

Courage

From choosing
the easier wrong decision
to making the tougher
right decision

Be strong and courageous. Do not be terrified;
do not be discouraged, for the Lord your God
will be with you wherever you go.

—Joshua 1:9

Issue: How do I do the right thing when I'm pressured to do otherwise?

Shutting my office door behind him, my boss said, "I think Mike has a nose problem. I heard that he's heavy into cocaine. I want you to get some dirt on the guy and fire him."

I was taken aback. Mike had been an excellent employee and one of my best salespeople for years. My first reaction was to do the right thing: I wanted to talk honestly to Mike. If, in fact, he did have a problem, I wanted to help him get his personal and professional life in order. But when I mentioned this approach to my boss, he blew up, saying, "I don't care how you do it, just get rid of him. I want him out of here now!"

I was caught between a rock and a hard place: I could do what was right and risk being fired myself, or I could choose not to make waves and be the team player as my boss would call it, and do the dirty work my boss had demanded I do. Well, I copped out and made the easier decision, the wrong one. I saved my job by unjustly taking the job of another. My boss's ego and my fear of unemployment hurt the entire staff. Not only did we lose a good employee, we also lost the trust of our sales team. The decision may have saved my job, but I lost a little piece of my soul.

Solution: Walk with God in courage.

A time will come when a leader's faith will be tested beyond his or her perceived limit, a time when business pressure, intellectual logic, and fear gang up on them, to the point where an easier wrong decision takes precedence over a tougher right decision. Fear and discouragement keep us from doing the right thing. Conversely, courage enables us to rise above difficulty to reach new heights as a leader. This is the time when leaders need to be strong and courageous and do what's right.

In this chapter, you'll read the stories of the Honorable Al Quie, former Governor of the State of Minnesota, and Marilyn Carlson Nelson, Chairman and CEO of Carlson Companies, an international hospitality company whose brands include Regent and Radisson Hotels, T.G.I. Friday's restaurants, and Carlson Wagonlit and Thomas Cook Travel. Although very different in position and circumstance, they learned that having the courage to do the right thing was a life-changing experience, not just for them, but for a greater good that at the time could only be seen by God.

AL QUIE

"Having the Courage to Walk Away"

The State of Minnesota was in serious financial difficulty. The tension and bitterness
between the Republicans and Democrats were at an all-time
high as they tried in vain to balance the budget. The battle
raged on for months as the recession of 1981 carried over
into January 1982. Everyone was worn out, especially the
leader, Republican Governor Al Quie.

Not only was Governor Quie tired of the battle with
the Democrats, he was tired of dealing with the press. In
reality, he knew he was avoiding the press because he was
hiding something deep within him and was not ready or
willing to confront it. "Every time a reporter asked me if I
was going to run for reelection, I would say 'yes,'" the
Governor recalls. "Each time I said 'yes,' I would feel a
sharp pain in my heart. I recognized that that happens
when I am not totally honest with myself."

Governor Quie remembers being particularly concerned
about a meeting he was to have on Friday with Betty, an outstanding reporter for the *Star & Tribune.* He knew that she
was good at going after the truth, and the Governor was not
ready to see her because he wasn't ready to talk about his

plans for reelection. "Even though I was telling people 'yes,' I wasn't at peace with that decision," says Governor Quie. "I was torn, and it was really affecting my mental health. Indecision has a debilitating effect on you. If you do what you don't believe, it will corrupt your soul. People in politics know what I am talking about. If enough people do it long enough, it will corrupt the whole institution."

As his appointment with Betty drew closer, Governor Quie felt increasingly uncomfortable. But as Friday morning approached, Governor Quie received the best news he had heard in a long time. The National Weather Service had posted a winter storm warning due to a severe blizzard that had developed in the northern plains and was bearing down on Minneapolis. Governor Quie made one swift and decisive move: He called Betty to postpone the interview until the following week.

He and his wife, Gretchen, quickly drove to their family farm nestled in the countryside near Marine on St. Croix, Minnesota. Governor Quie explained, "The most satisfying feeling in a person is to be totally honest. In politics, many times you can't tell people right away; you need to sort things out first. I absolutely did *not* want to see Betty. I knew this blizzard would give me an opportunity to get away from the bombarding of my world and be alone in the presence of God."

Retreating to the family farm during this snowstorm brought back some of Governor Quie's cherished memories. "I love blizzards," he says. In fact, one of his clearest memories is of a time when he was walking in the woods by his family's farm. Howling winds and blinding snow nearly swallowed him as he walked. But when he got deep into the woods, everything became quiet and still. He recalls, "I remember looking up and seeing the blizzard raging through the treetops, but the trees protected me from the wind. There I experienced total peace and quiet. The snow fell gently down as the blizzard raged fiercely above. It was awesome! It was like being in the hands of God with the world raging around you." That memory has kept him grounded in some turbulent times, and it gave him courage in this one.

As Governor Quie settled into a weekend of being quiet and listening to God, he played out the pros and cons of running for reelection. He quickly came to the realization that there actually was no dilemma. The solution had been there all along, but he hadn't really accepted it. Governor Quie knew in his heart that he wasn't going to run for reelection. He admits, "I hadn't had the courage to do the right thing. Fear and ego got in the way."

Still, he wasn't sure how to tell people that he wasn't running again. He was no quitter, but stepping out of office could make him look like one. Governor Quie explains, "When you say 'I'm not going to run anymore,' people will say, 'He couldn't take it, he's out of here!' When a person trains himself to be macho, be strong, be a man, face dangers, not show weakness, be in control, how do you let go of that?"

When the time came, the Governor found two scriptures that helped him clarify his decision not to run for reelection. In John 6:28–29, after the people had asked Jesus, "What must we do to do the works God requires?," Jesus answered, "The work of God is this: to believe in the one he has sent," and in Mark 10:45, Governor Quie also saw how Jesus came "not to be served, but to serve."

Considering those scriptures showed the Governor that his ego and busyness were getting in the way of him being in tune to God. He realized that if he ran for reelection, he would be serving his ego rather than serving the greater good. "I was raised with the idea of helping other people," says Governor Quie. He quickly realized that he could do more good for the people of Minnesota if he didn't run for reelection. Partisan politics often keeps sides from working together, and the Governor had a glimmer of hope that by foregoing another term in office, he could work with the Democratic leader of the state to help the people of Minnesota. "What I did know was as long as I was running, there was no way they would work with me," he recalls. "To the Democrats, I was the enemy; they would prove they won by making sure I lost."

By the end of the weekend, Governor Quie was comfortable with his decision and had mustered the courage to do the right thing. It was time to announce that he was not running for reelection. Governor Quie looked around him. The Twin Cities were beautiful after the big snowstorm. The sky was a deep blue, the air was fresh and crisp, and the entire city had a fresh blanket of pure white. There was an unmistakable newness and freshness about it. And that's exactly how he felt on Monday, January 26, 1982, as he announced that he would not seek reelection for Governor of Minnesota.

"I was free!" he says. "From the moment I made my decision, my judgment was never again colored by my concern for reelection."

Governor Quie received another benefit that he never dreamed would happen. After his decision, people saw him in a different light. His credibility went up because people sensed that he had sacrificed his career for a greater good, for their good. As the former governor explains, "You can't say it, think it, plot it, or plan it. People see the true spirit of service when it comes from your heart."

A shift in focus to the higher good broke the logjam of even the most bitter political battle. Governor Quie's courage to let go of his power and ego allowed others to break down similar barriers. The budget battle stalemate, which had brewed for months, was resolved in three days.

Simply put, the leaders had to find ways to cut spending and had to find an acceptable way to raise taxes. The Republicans were adamantly against raising taxes, while the Democrats didn't want to cut spending. In April 1982, Governor Quie called each Republican and Democratic leader from the House and Senate and met with them personally. He told them that he wanted to have a private meeting with the key leaders to resolve the budget. Then he asked them to pick all the necessary decision-makers so the hard decisions could be made at the meeting.

Many of the leaders were hesitant because all meetings were to be "open meetings," open to the press. Governor Quie tells us, "I explained to them that if we brought in the press, the focus would be on looking good in the public eye, rather than having the courage to do what's best and right for the public." This time they met without the press.

With Governor Quie's new courage and conviction, he helped each leader find the courage to focus on the higher good. Understanding the political risks he was asking each leader to take, Governor Quie offered himself as a buffer. He told them, "If you feel a decision is too dangerous politically, you can blame me."

That eventful meeting started Monday morning. By Wednesday night, both houses of the legislature had passed the bill to resolve the budget shortfall. By November 1982, the severe national recession caused them to do it again: They were able to put a system in place that showed an estimated $500 million surplus for the State of Minnesota. In reality, it turned out to be a surplus closer to $1 billion.

It's so easy to get bombarded with the noise of our circumstances. Not only are we pressured into decisions by others, but the voice of our ego also deafens our ability to hear God's whisper. It takes courage to listen to God with a totally honest heart. It takes even greater courage to follow through on what we hear. In Governor Quie's case, he learned that it wasn't about choosing a right or wrong decision; it was about having the courage to see and follow through with the decision that had been whispering in his heart all along.

MARILYN CARLSON NELSON
"Having the Courage to Overcome Tragedy"

Marilyn Nelson had the life many people strive for. The eldest daughter of Curt Carlson, founder and Chairman of Carlson Companies, Marilyn had wealth, influence, strong faith, a good marriage, a loving family, and an active professional and community life. Everything appeared to be going well until an eventful day: October 3, 1985. Her busy day at Carlson Companies was interrupted by the call that is every parent's worst nightmare: Her beloved 19-year-old-daughter, Juliet, had been killed in an automobile accident.

Marilyn's world immediately spun out of control and crashed. "Even though I had a powerful faith, it was devastating," Marilyn explained. It is hard to imagine a tougher challenge than facing the loss of a loved one. As many people experience, at first, Marilyn was angry at God. Then she denied that God even existed, struggling painfully with how a good God can let something like this happen.

But after all the wrestling about Juliet's death—a very natural grieving process—Marilyn tried desperately to make sense of the situation. She read the Bible and many other kinds of books and listened to different philosophers.

But when all the voices on the pages and platforms were silent, she still had no answers—just more questions.

Marilyn tells people, "I knew I could choose to give up and put the pillow over my head, or I could fight back. I knew my options of becoming 'bitter or better' and wanted to learn from this experience. I never gave up. I continued to search, ask, and knock, and eventually the door got opened again. Slowly but surely, I gained insights that helped me heal and get better."

She explains that one of those moments came from reading the story in the Bible about the talents. In this story, a master goes away and asks his servants to invest their talents. While most of us see this as a metaphor for using our God-given talents, Marilyn found, through Juliet's death, that this was also a parable about time. "The only time we have is today," says Marilyn. "We should live each day as our signature day. We may have ten thousand days remaining, or it could be our last. If this day stood for all of time, is this a day you would want to have your name on?"

Out of the ruins of despair, Marilyn rebuilt her life, one moment at a time, one decision at a time, one day at a time. She tells others that leadership is about making decisions every day. She knows well that leaders regularly are faced with making compromises and that it becomes easy to rationalize those compromises. To Marilyn, true leadership is found not only in making the big decisions, but also (and perhaps even more so) in the little decisions that must be made every day. Those decisions prove one's greatness.

As painful as Juliet's death was, it helped Marilyn grow. "It gave me perspective," she says. "Once you lose something unspeakable, a loss you think you couldn't sustain, and you survive it, other problems change in their perspective. For me, time and relationships are really precious."

Marilyn has grown stronger from adversity. It was a slow process of living a moment and a day at a time. She likes to remind people that none of us knows what is waiting in the next chapter of life. Every single day is important. We learn to take responsibility, yet stay open to seeing, hearing, and sensing God's direction.

After her daughter's death, Marilyn began to see little messages of hope coming her way day after day. More and more, she sensed God at work in her life. One day her sister came to see her and, instead of having a good visit, they got into a painful conflict. Marilyn's sister, though trying to be supportive, told Marilyn to get on with her life. All of the emotions Marilyn had been carrying inside welled up and poured out. "I let her have it," recalls Marilyn. "I yelled and screamed at her and ran into my bedroom. I got into bed and fell asleep." Several hours later Marilyn woke up and went into the living room. Her sister was still there, sitting on the couch. When Marilyn asked her why she was still there, her sister calmly answered, "I was just waiting here until you woke up." That was a powerful, hope-filled moment as Marilyn deeply felt her sister's love toward her. Marilyn strongly sensed, "God is at work here."

Since then, Marilyn's strength has grown one day at a time in spite of continued trials and setbacks. In 1999, Marilyn's father, Curt Carlson, passed away. His death, like her daughter's, did not ultimately overcome her. Instead, it strengthened her to lead Carlson Companies into the new century.

Curt Carlson came from a background where money was scarce. His family lived in Sweden during the potato famine. Curt's father, Marilyn's grandfather, came to the United States, and Curt grew up learning that making money was very important. His life was about accumulating enough financial capital to be successful.

But Marilyn, never burdened with such a fear of scarcity, was passionate about people: attracting and nurturing *human* capital. As the leader of Carlson Companies, she wants to empower people to do more together than they can do alone. She believes that God is at the core of relationships. By allowing God a place at work, people would be encouraged to find and utilize their talents. They begin to believe they can make a difference. Leaders need to create the environment that allows this to happen.

I asked Marilyn what she would want stated as her epitaph. She answered by quoting Isaiah 40:29–31: "He gives strength to the weary and increases power to the weak. Even youths grow tired and weary, and young men stumble and fall; but those who hope in the Lord will renew their strength. They will soar on wings like eagles; they will run and not grow weary, they will walk and not be faint."

What is her advice for people who are struggling in pain or experiencing burnout? "You are not alone, God is with you," she offers. "There are little messages of hope that are out there. If you let them in, they will rekindle your hope and spirit." And Marilyn herself is a message of hope to those who know her.

CONCLUSION

Courage is easily misunderstood. For many, courage is defined by doing bold or brave things. The underlying reason for the action may be ego gratification, power, or recognition. Demonstrating moral courage is very much a private matter between you and God. Sometimes, as with Governor Quie, we come to a point where we know God is calling us to change our life's direction, and we must quiet our ego in order to hear God's whisper. Sometimes, like Marilyn Carlson Nelson, we are confronted with a painful blow that shakes the very foundations of our beliefs and we need the courage to renew and deepen our faith in God.

Whatever your situation, you (like these leaders) will probably be brought to a special place of tested faith and courage, a place where you will be challenged to go against the grain of common sense to move into the uncharted waters of illogical faith. Common challenges, rewards, and blessings occur for all of us who have the choice to do the right thing.

1. Common Challenges

Both Governor Quie and Marilyn Carlson Nelson struggled intensely before finding the courage to move on with a new life. Whether the consequences they pictured were real or imagined, they both faced fear and discouragement. In Governor Quie's case, he feared ending his political career and being labeled as a quitter. In Marilyn's situation, her loss was devastating and her discouragement was enormous. Although public figures, they each had to take a private journey to reexamine their faith in God.

Both consciously came to a point where they subordinated their desires for a higher purpose and a greater good. Governor Quie put the citizens of Minnesota ahead of his career while Marilyn turned her energy to serving her employees and community. Both came to a point where their trust in God transcended their present circumstances, and they took a leap of faith.

2. Common Rewards and Blessings

Governor Quie and Marilyn Carlson Nelson each were given significant power and authority. These case studies provide an excellent reminder that power and authority have little to do with money and position and everything to do with character and aligning your actions with your principles. Governor Quie accomplished more in his final year as Governor and beyond because his actions expressed his desire to serve the greater good of the State. Marilyn's influence and authority is now based on her renewed faith and courage to overcome personal tragedy, rather than the leadership inherited from a famous father. Their personal decisions have benefited countless people.

Most of our lives are shaped by the small decisions we make every day. It doesn't matter whether the decision we're faced with is big or small. What's important is to understand that every decision helps shape our character and destiny. We are either becoming who we want to be or who God wants us to be. Business demands, coupled with personal fears and ego, make choosing the wrong decision tempting. For that reason alone, it is even more important to take time to make sure our decisions align with our faith, values, and principles. It is wise to prayerfully consider God's counsel for all of our decisions. Asking ourselves these two questions will help guide us when choices must be made:

What is the right thing to do?
Am I willing to trust God's promise that He is with me in this decision, regardless of the consequences?

Deciding what is right and acting on our convictions can be a daunting task. We are all different people with many different situations. We may never understand why God has placed a certain decision before us. Nevertheless, the one thing we have in common is that God has promised that He is with us *always*.

DISCUSSION GUIDE

Part 1: Individuals facing a difficult decision

1. What is the most difficult decision you are facing?
2. What are your fears and concerns regarding this dilemma?
3. What do you believe God is saying to you about this decision?
4. In your opinion, what do you think is the easier wrong decision?
5. What are the consequences and implications of making the easier decision?
6. What do you think is the right thing to do?
7. What are the consequences and implications of making the right decision?

Part 2: Individuals facing a difficult situation

1. How do you cope with your present situation?
2. What attitudes do you presently battle with?
3. How can you develop the patience to wait for God's answers?
4. What gives you comfort during this difficult period?
5. What messages of hope can you see?
6. How can you move forward with courage to transcend this difficulty?

4

Patience

From sprinting under pressure
to running with purpose

*Let us run with perseverance
the race marked out for us.*

–Hebrews 12:1

Issue: How do I avoid becoming a slave to urgent, short-term pressure?

The corporate office was breathing down our necks. We had only 45 days to achieve our fourth-quarter goal, or else. Our sales team had spent months developing a meaningful strategic plan. In that plan, our long-term goal was to build a base of loyal, long-term customers. We thought we were in the clear to work our plan, but that went out the window with a business shortfall in the third quarter. This downturn created the same old battle cry: Stop what you are doing! We need to create a short-term plan for business now!

We paid less attention to our existing customers so we could focus on getting immediate new business. The good news is we won the short-term battle. We achieved our fourth-quarter goal. The bad news is we lost the war. In the process of "doing whatever it takes" to achieve our short-term objective, we completely lost focus of our long-term goal.

We were so focused on the short-term bottom line that we lost focus on the overall plan. We asked our customers to accommodate our needs, and in the process lost focus of their needs. We were so busy getting new customers that we left our existing customers feeling unwanted, unappreciated, and used. While we fervently sought new business in the short term, two of our biggest and most loyal customers quietly let their contracts expire and went to a competitor.

Solution: Develop patience to run a long-distance race in a 100-yard dash world.

Patience and bottom-line pressure are like oil and water. They don't mix. Having the patience to work a long-term plan sounds great in theory, but, in reality, short-term pressure often forces us to play another game. Pressure comes from both external and internal forces. The bottom line expectation to produce, coupled with our internal pressure to succeed, takes us out of our game plan. We exhaust our energies sprinting from quarter to quarter, running a race dictated by pressure. With patience, we learn to run the race we have been called to run, in spite of the pressure that surrounds us.

In this chapter we will meet two leaders with a common trait, patience. Tony Dungy, Head Coach of the Tampa Bay Buccaneers football team, transcended the outside pressure to produce. Archie Dunham, Chairman and CEO of Conoco Inc., an oil industry leader, transcended his internal pressure to succeed. Both leaders discovered that patience is the key to long-term success.

TONY DUNGY

"Pressure from the Outside: Sticking to God's Plan Produces Results"

The Tampa Bay Buccaneers walked dejectedly back to the locker room. The pressure was growing after another heartbreaking loss. Their 1996 NFL season was now an awful 0-5! The pressure to win grew stronger with each loss. Patience was growing thin. The players were discouraged and frustrated. The fans were tired of losing and wanted to see a winner. The media fanned the flames of discontent claiming "same old Bucs— same old losers." The owners were remaining supportive but were quietly nervous. They wanted financial support committed to the building of a new stadium; losing the first five games was not going to help build a stadium. There was pressure to make a change . . . any change. Advice began to roll in from all sides. Change the quarterback! Run more! Pass more! Change the defense! Change the coaching staff! Coming from all over, the pressure pointed to one person: the new head coach, Tony Dungy.

To say that Tony Dungy had considerable pressure to produce would be an understatement. It took him 15 years to become a head coach in the NFL. He was only the fourth black head coach in NFL history. Upon finally receiving his big opportunity, he was immediately surrounded by impatient Tampa Bay players, fans, owners, and community. "When are you going to win?" "How will you win?" "What changes are you going to make to win?"

Turning to Tony, what did all these desperate eyes see as they looked at this pressured person? Panic? Anger? Desperation? No. They saw a calm, patient leader who was keenly aware of his circumstances, yet was unwilling to allow short-term defeat to get in the way of his long-term plan for success. Tony recalls, "I was disappointed, but not discouraged. I prayed, 'Lord, you brought us here for a reason. You have something in store for us.' I felt our situation would make our story even better." Tony believed that God had a greater plan that transcended winning and losing.

To gain insight into Tony's patience and perseverance, it's important to understand a little more about his journey. When Tony was 21 years old, he was a rookie with the Pittsburgh Steelers, a young man who dreamed of becoming a successful player in the National Football League. He had been a star quarterback at the University of Minnesota, where he had twice been named Most Valuable Player. Football was his top priority.

"Everything was going well," recalls Tony, "when I suddenly became sick with mononucleosis and was unable to play. The illness lingered for six weeks. I grew frustrated and impatient, not being able to do anything other than just wait."

Tony voiced his frustrations to his roommate, Donnie Shell. Donnie's response cut right to the heart of the matter. He turned to the impatient young man and said, "Football is the most important thing in your life, and God wants to see if that is above Him or below Him. Until you are ready to put football below Him, you will always be frustrated with your problems." Donnie's comments made Tony take a look at himself and his priorities.

From that point on, Tony placed his football career in God's hands. His favorite Bible verse, Proverbs 16:3, demonstrates that the key to Tony's patience lies where he places his faith. "Commit to the Lord whatever you do and your plans will succeed." Tony's career and success have been built not only on seeking God's will and timing, but also in patiently working God's long-term plan in a business with short-term goals.

After his playing career ended, Tony moved into coaching. He patiently waited for the opportunity to become an NFL head coach. Though a highly successful defensive coordinator/assistant coach with the Minnesota Vikings, he was continuously overlooked as a potential head coach. In 1993 the Vikings had the number-one defense, seven head coach jobs were vacant, and Tony wasn't offered even one of the opportunities.

NFL owners, on the whole, desire a coach with one thing on his mind—winning. As a prospective coach, Tony didn't have that mind set. While interviewing with respective owners, he openly shared his values. "While winning is important, it should be a result of doing what's right," he told them. He wanted to win, too, but believed in a long-term goal, one that transcended winning and losing. His goal was to develop his players to become not only the best they were capable of becoming, but also to be good community citizens and role models for today's youth. Tony's beliefs and values may have cost him job opportunities, but he was at peace. He recalls, "I was comfortable waiting for the right opportunity. I had faith that the Lord would place me where I was supposed to be."

Tony received his big break in 1996 when he became the head coach of the Tampa Bay Bucs. "I believe I'm in Tampa because it's God's plan," says Tony. Clearly, he didn't set out to get the job, and he didn't move heaven and earth to get there. In fact, the owners were looking for a high-profile coach, and Tony didn't fit that description. Jimmy Johnson was the first choice, but he turned down the offer to go to Miami. University of Florida head coach Steve Spurier was the second choice; however, he chose to stay at the university. Knowing he wasn't a top choice, Tony's attitude remained peaceful: "If it's the Lord's will, I will get the job, and, if not, life goes on," he told himself.

When he interviewed for the Bucs' head coach position, he was completely honest. "I never sacrificed my integrity," says Tony. "I shared everything, including my view on winning, my faith, my leadership style, and my desire for the Bucs to become role models and good community citizens. We openly discussed the expectations we had of each other. I have a responsibility to respond to their authority, yet in the things under my authority, I have to do what I believe is right. They respected what I stood for and gave me full support."

Tony was excited about the owner's willingness to support his long-term plan, but he also knew he had his work cut out for him. The Bucs had built one main reputation since their first season in 1976: They were losers. They carried a bad reputation on and off the field. Tony inherited a team with a track record of losing, having poor attitudes, and maintaining only low expectations.

One of the first things Tony Dungy did was to build a coaching staff of men who shared his values of character, personal accountability, and teamwork. The coaches and senior players were given the role of helping younger players become all they were capable of becoming, both on and off the field. From the beginning, Tony set up a system for the older players to help the younger players. He told them, "It's your responsibility to counsel the younger guys." Tony was certain that leadership by example, accountability, and unselfish teamwork would lead to long-term success for the Bucs and for the players themselves.

Tony explains that at the first meeting on the first day of training camp, they talked about the high standards of their game plan and the high expectations of each individual on the team. He defined success as "doing the very best you are capable of doing." Of course, it's good when that translates into wins, playoffs, and a Superbowl, but no such outcome is guaranteed. "If all we think about are Superbowls and winning," says Tony, "then we will compromise and take our focus off being the best we can be. I talked to every player on the team. I asked each one to be a part of the solution. Help us set a new direction. I told them, 'The guys that handle responsibility will be successful. The more we accept personal responsibility and help each other, the quicker we will achieve our success. Now, let's all be accountable to each other.'"

Tony's long-term plan was challenged when the team stumbled to a disastrous 0-5 start. But the new coach's steady perseverance was reassuring. He didn't point fingers or place blame. Instead he told them that he was not looking to make quick changes but was going to solve the problems. After each loss, they reviewed the things they did wrong and made the necessary adjustments for improvement. "The losing streak was difficult, but I saw how the players were growing," Tony recalls.

Tony modeled everything he stood for. In the midst of adversity, he modeled the character and patience he wanted in his players. He had been on a losing team. As a young player on the San Francisco 49ers, Tony watched head coach Bill Walsh. They lost their first seven games, but three years later the team was in the Superbowl. Tony knew it was crucial for him to be a model of patience and consistency in the midst of defeat.

Coach Dungy knew his patience had made an impact when Dave Moore, a tight end, came to him after the first season. Dave told Tony, "The whole team, including me, was waiting to see you just lose it. Nobody can go through this and be the same. We were all waiting for you to go off on us." He didn't.

Today, the Tampa Bay Bucs represent a different kind of success story. In the NFL, success is still defined by winning. With just a few years under Tony's leadership, the Tampa Bay Bucs became winners, the 1999 NFL Central Division Champions. But this is a success story that transcends winning football games, and the Bucs are much more than an NFL title. The players have become wonderful role models, and the Tampa Bay community loves them. Attendance in their new stadium is at an all-time high.

Tony Dungy believes that even when success is delayed, patience is ultimately rewarded, even in a business that is so demanding. "When you have success, it is easy to stick with your convictions," explains Tony. "But when success is delayed, to stick with what you believe is right is difficult. I believe patience is rewarded. God works in ways that appear to be illogical. You have to be willing to stick with God's plan even when you don't understand it."

When people associated with football are asked to describe Tony Dungy, the words *patience, commitment,* and *consistency* come up with regularity. As a result of his character, Tony Dungy has become one of the most loved and respected coaches in the NFL.

ARCHIE DUNHAM

"Pressure from the Inside: Trusting in God's Plan Prepares You for Success"

Archie Dunham was bright, ambitious, and frustrated. At the age of 36, a middle manager for Conoco Inc., he felt he had plateaued. "I was impatient," he says of that time. "Things were not moving fast enough for me." Though doing well at Conoco, his impatience made him restless and unhappy.

While living in Houston, Archie became an active member of Spring Baptist Church. The church was rapidly growing and needed land to expand. The pastor asked Archie if he would chair a committee to negotiate with seven physicians who jointly owned the land south of the church. Archie agreed to chair the committee, and, in his typical management style, picked the highest powered and brightest business executives, lawyers, and developers to be on the committee. The final committee member was an elderly deacon, Luther. For the most part, the committee members were young, bright business executives. Then there was Luther, a man of God who was twice the age of every other member.

Archie felt the assignment would be quick and easy. He thought, "Piece of cake. With the level of talent and skill the committee possessed, the deal will be negotiated in no time." In reality, negotiations broke down quickly with little progress made. After each negotiation session, the committee would regroup and revise its strategy. Following each meeting, Luther politely asked Archie the same question, "Archie, are you seeking God's help with this problem or are you trying to solve it yourself?" Each time, Archie replied, "Of course I'm seeking God's direction." Inwardly, he knew he wasn't. Six weeks later, Archie finally allowed God control of the situation. To his amazement, the problem was quickly resolved, and the physicians agreed to sell the land.

Later that year, relaxing on the swing in his backyard, he realized that he had turned his salvation over to God but never turned over control of his life and career. The revelation of his lack of trust humbled him. There on that swing, Archie prayed, "Lord, if you want me to live in hot, humid Houston for the next 30 years, if you want me to stay in this job for the next 30 years, I will do it if that's the plan you have for me." That brief moment on the swing changed Archie's destiny, because finally Archie completely gave up control of his career. From that moment came a meteoric rise from a frustrated middle manager to Chairman of the Board and CEO of Conoco Inc. He listened for God's will and he had the faith to trust in God's plan.

Six months after he accepted the idea of living in hot and humid Houston, if that was God's desire for him, Archie was transferred to cool and beautiful Newport Beach, California, as Executive Vice President for a Conoco subsidiary, a job he never imagined having. Archie and his family loved their new environment. He enjoyed his new responsibility, and his family enjoyed living in San Clemente.

Two years later, Archie received a call from the President of Conoco. The President told him that Conoco's headquarters was going to move from downtown Houston to the suburbs. More importantly, he wanted Archie to be the Project Manager. Remembering the lesson he learned on his swing, he told the President he needed to think about it. After much prayer, Archie felt that God was telling him to remain in California. He called and respectfully declined. He recalls, "Fifteen seconds after turning down the offer, I began to get calls from all my former bosses who were now Vice Presidents of the corporation. They exclaimed, 'Have you lost your mind?' and 'This is a great opportunity! We called the President and said that you were a bit hasty and needed another week to think about the offer.'" Archie agreed and decided to pray for guidance again. This time, he was even more convinced to stay in California and turn down the job opportunity in Houston. Six months later, Archie was named President of the Conoco subsidiary.

Over the years, Archie remained steadfast in his commitment to follow God's career path for him. However, it wasn't always easy. He still struggled with his impatience from time to time. Archie recalled a fairly recent time when he once again grew frustrated and impatient to move up the corporate ladder. About that time, he received a call from a prestigious Board Search Committee inquiring to see if he was interested in becoming the CEO of one of the largest Fortune 100 companies in the country. "It was everything I dreamed about," Archie says. "It offered a great challenge, a nice city to live in, and a fantastic compensation package." He was excited to pursue the job, but didn't have total clarity about the move. He valued his long tenure with Conoco, yet was intrigued by this enticing offer. Once again, he prayed. Finally, he said, "Lord, I am going to leave Conoco unless you stop me." Eight hours later, he received a call from the Chairman of the Search Committee. They had placed the search on hold. Archie felt wonderful! He knew this was a tremendous confirmation to stay at Conoco.

Six weeks later, he received a call at 5:00 A.M. from the Chairman of DuPont, Conoco's parent company at the time. His boss quickly stated, "Wake up and brush your teeth! I'll call you back in 10 minutes to discuss something important with you." Ten minutes later, Archie was named President and CEO of Conoco Inc.

On May 11, 1998, the *Wall Street Journal* announced that Conoco Inc., and its parent company, DuPont, were going to separate, making it the largest initial public offering in U.S. corporate history. That announcement set in motion a series of events that created the most stressful time in Archie Dunham's life.

The initial public offering of Conoco totaled $4.4 billion. The resulting dilemma weighed heavily on Archie. "We had a fiduciary responsibility to entertain offers from third parties to acquire all of the company," explains Archie. "As a member of the DuPont Board, my role was to evaluate all offers, but in my heart, I wanted Conoco to be a separate company because I knew it would be best for Conoco's employees. It was extremely stressful. We knew that we could choose to accept an offer from a 'super major' oil company and find ourselves no longer part of DuPont but part of another company instead. That would mean Conoco being broken into pieces, with thousands of employees being laid off and management being terminated." This was the ultimate test of faith for Archie. As he humorously recalls, "Before that, I had blond hair; now it's gray."

Once again Archie found himself in the kind of situation in which he first turned his career over to God. He and his wife tried to get away from the stress. On August 30, 1998, Archie and his wife went to Colorado for a four-day vacation, but they had no rest. The fax machine kept printing out new offers. Walking into the backyard, he found himself in a familiar setting. Sitting on the swing, he struggled between his will and God's will. His greatest concern was for the thousands of Conoco employees, yet he knew he had to honor his fiduciary responsibility to evaluate third party offers to the best of his ability. It boiled down to

Archie's will for Conoco versus God's will for Conoco. "I had to totally trust that His outcome would be the best for me, my management team, and our employees," Archie recalls. "I came to the deep understanding that God's will was the perfect solution for me, for the company, and for Conoco's employees. Finally, I was ready to accept His outcome for our company. I was at peace."

The Conoco initial public offering was the largest and most successful in the history of the New York Stock Exchange. In the end, everyone won. By mid 1999 the value of Conoco stock had increased 50%, as compared to 20% for the oil industry and 6% in the S&P 500 since the start of 1999. Management remains intact and ready to take on the challenge of growing the company to double its present value by the year 2003. Employees have kept their jobs and enjoyed the stability provided by Archie's leadership.

And Archie himself? To corporate America, Archie is a hero. *Forbes* magazine recently showered praise on him. *Forbes* stated that Conoco, which had rated dead last among the top 14 oil companies in 1992, is now ranked first in the Schroder & Company's annual ranking for exploration and production performance between 1994–1998, leading its peers in profits per barrel.

While Archie's story may say "turn your career over to God and you'll be successful," there is another, more significant message. Following God's plan is the ultimate win-win solution. Of course, we don't use God for our success; He utilizes our talents for His success. God often chooses to work through those people He can depend on. Those who are faithful with a little are given more. But we also enjoy the benefits of following His plan. In the process of fulfilling God's will, we grow stronger in character and more capable in tough situations. He tests us through challenging circumstances to see if we have the character and capability to follow Him. While difficult for us, this is an extremely important time in which God is shaping us into unity with His purpose. It is no coincidence that this powerful combination of character and capability grooms us for success in the business world.

In Archie's case, God was preparing him to handle the Conoco initial public offering. The raises and promotions were by-products of following God's plan. It took 25 years of testing and refining to prepare Archie for the important role he played in Conoco's sale and future.

Archie Dunham is a leader with 25 years of training in patience. He was forced to think through the moral, ethical, and financial implications of an important decision that affected thousands of lives. Archie Dunham is where he is because he has followed God's plan and has provided value to others. In the same way, when we have the patience and courage to follow God's perfect plan in obedience, we too become more valuable to others.

Archie is no longer impatient. Now he is passionate about sharing his message of trusting God's perfect plan. He tells people how important it is to trust the Lord in all their major decisions and to be patient. While God doesn't promise that someone will be financially successful, He does promise to provide His best outcome. Says Archie, "Some choose at 30 to follow His plan; some people wait until they are 60 years old; some never do it. I think those who go their own way miss out on what God's perfect plan is for their life." Archie was willing to trust God, and, as a result, he is happier and healthier than his plans would ever have led him to be.

CONCLUSION

Tony Dungy and Archie Dunham demonstrate the patience to run a different type of race, one in which they allow God's timing to set the pace. They each demonstrate their ability to persevere in running the race God has marked out for them. They were both steadfast and consistent in working with a purpose in spite of difficulties and pressure. These two men relied on three traits that helped them succeed through patience and perseverance.

1. Prayer

Both men used prayer as a means to overcome impatience. In Tony's situation, it gave him the strength to hold on to his plan in spite of outside pressure. In Archie's case, it helped him let go of his impatience to climb the corporate ladder.

For both, it was the most practical tool they used for making tough decisions. As leaders, they were bombarded with advice from all sides. Their consistent communication with God kept them focused on their main purpose, rather than distracted by the immediate obstacles in their path.

2. Perspective

I'll always remember the insightful words of my friend Andy Anderson. He said, "Larry, your problem is that you have blinders on. You are so focused on the bottom line, you can't see the world around you." He was absolutely right. I associated our sales team with a greyhound dog race. We all ran as fast as we could to catch the rabbit. Nothing else came into our sights except our goal. We sprinted from goal to goal but had no sense of purpose. In reality, we were just running in circles.

Goal achievement is extremely important, but it's easy to lose perspective. Our sales team expended all its energy trying to feed the insatiable quarterly revenue god, promotion god, and personal security god, and it was never enough. Over time, we eventually became slaves to short-term goals, living our lives from quarter to quarter.

Both Tony Dungy and Archie Dunham had perspective. They both saw a bigger picture in the midst of their circumstances, and this helped them work within their purpose. Perspective gave them a context from which to make sound decisions. Perspective helped them see a higher purpose in their work that transcended their immediate problems. Tony saw his losing streak as an opportunity to build character in his players. Archie learned how to wait on God, rather than jump at the first promotion that came his way. Perspective helped these men set the pace of their race rather than letting their circumstances set the pace.

3. Preparation

Both Tony and Archie relied on patience and perseverance as a necessary instrument for growth. In essence, their patience was preparing them for greater service to God. The long distance runner gains success by gaining endurance. Endurance helps the long distance runner grow stronger by increasing his or her capacity to run, often by weathering pain. In the same way, the more Tony and Archie practiced running with perseverance instead of caving under pressure, the better prepared they became for the next circumstance, the next challenge, and the next opportunity.

We live in an impatient world. The business world has trained us to run the 100-yard dash, where success is measured in terms of tangible results such as speed to market, sales, profit/loss, and market share. While these goals are necessary and important, the challenge is in following God's plan when the business world demands we react quickly to another plan. Often, God's plan seems to make no sense in a business environment because we try to measure God's plan using the same tangible measurements we use to determine our business success. Ultimately, winning the marathon instead of the 100-yard dash comes down to two questions: What kind of race do we want to run? Who is setting the pace?

As Rousseau stated, "Patience is bitter, but its fruit is sweet." Many of us struggle with patience because it's so hard to see any immediate benefit. God's perfect plan for our life may not involve tangible evidence today. Often, it's the things we can't see in the present that prepare us for a significant future. But we can run boldly and with perseverance the race that God has specially marked out for each of us.

DISCUSSION GUIDE

1. What is the greatest external pressure you face?
2. What is the greatest internal pressure you feel?
3. Describe the ideal pace of your professional life. Your personal life?
4. What prevents you from working at the pace you desire?
5. What can you do to run the race God has marked out for you?

Leadership by Example

From what you do to who you are

Let your light shine before men,
that they may see your good deeds
and praise your Father in heaven.

–Matthew 5:16

Issue:

How do I demonstrate my faith in a politically correct and diverse work environment?

I was walking home from school with my friend, Freddie, who was also Jewish, when two tough-looking teenage boys came up to us. One of them turned to Freddie and said, "Hey, kid, are you Jewish?" Freddie, looking down, quietly said, "No." Then the stranger turned to me and asked the same question. "Hey, kid, are you Jewish?" I looked up and innocently answered, "Yes." Then to my shock, the teenager spit in my face. I couldn't figure out why he would single me out and spit in my face. It didn't take long to convince myself that it's not a good idea to reveal your religious beliefs. It's best to keep them to yourself.

Many years later, I developed a personal relationship with Jesus Christ. Even so, I still didn't want to share my faith with others. I hadn't liked being labeled as a Jew, and I did not want to be labeled as a born-again Christian. I had carried that lesson through my childhood and the beginning of my business career. Being quiet about one's faith in the workplace made perfect sense. Why would I reveal my faith and risk my career?

Solution: Let who you are speak for what you believe.

Sharing one's faith at work is a highly sensitive area and rightly so. Revealing your inner faith invites stereotyping, defensiveness, and debates about political correctness, not to mention the legal implications.

On the other hand, we don't want to hide the very essence of who we are. There is nothing wrong with revealing the source of our values, decisions, and priorities. In fact, integrating our faith and work paves the way to a more meaningful and productive work environment. This chapter is not about whether we are allowed to bring our religion to work. This is not a debate on whether God should be at our workplace. God is in our workplace! God doesn't wait for us at the end of the day to see how our day was in the secular world. He is with us wherever we go. Integrating work and faith is about bringing who we are to work.

To help us gain perspective on this very personal dilemma, we'll read the stories of two leaders who have struggled with this issue. Jeff Coors, former President of Adolph Coors Brewing Company, and John Beckett, President, R. W. Beckett Corporation, a manufacturer of residential oil furnaces and author of *Loving Monday: Succeeding in Business Without Selling Your Soul,* have found integrating work and faith is a challenging, meaningful, and rewarding experience.

JEFFREY H. COORS
"Moving from Doing for God to Being with God"

Twenty-five years ago, Jeff Coors was a young, aggressive junior executive well on his way to taking over his father's and uncle's roles as leaders of Adolph Coors Brewing Company. Although his career was on the right track, he was struggling in his spiritual life. He had been a church attendee his whole life, but it wasn't until August 1974 that Jeff developed a deep personal relationship with God.

"It was the first time in my life that I had a clear understanding of how biblical principles applied to my life. My immediate desire was to apply these principles at work," Jeff explains. Jeff quickly realized he was caught between two worlds: It was okay to discuss biblical principles with church members on Sunday, but it was taboo to discuss them at work Monday through Friday. Jeff recalls, "I felt very lonely. My pastor had no experience to give advice in this area, and my fellow Christians felt that work and faith should be separate."

As he continued to grow in his understanding of the power behind biblical principles, Jeff continued to wrestle with how best to reconcile his spiritual self with his business self. Being open about his faith was both risky and frightening, considering he came from a public family that ran a public company.

To compound his split-identity issues, Jeff, like many so many executives, was a doer. He was an action-oriented and goal-driven self-starter. While Jeff loved God and wanted to do His will in business, Jeff's will and determination got in the way. "I was just so zealous for doing things for God," Jeff says. But he found that when he tried to do the work of the Lord, he tended to get ahead of God rather than being led by Him. Jeff used the force of his own will to get things done. For example, zealous to be a peacemaker, Jeff interpreted that to mean making others be peaceful— bumping heads and forcing the peace.

Jeff continued to struggle with finding the right way to integrate his faith and work until 1989, when things came to a head. He felt he had reached a position of power and status to do great things for God, but he was not at peace. Now the President of Adolph Coors Brewing Company, he was a powerful local, state, and national leader. And he was incredibly over-committed.

Before he realized it, Jeff found himself over-involved and way over-extended. As President of the Adolph Coors Company, he was managing the beer business, ceramics business, and a dozen other owned businesses. Jeff was on a dozen boards, leading a business project in Denver called Blueprint for Colorado, and starting a Christian prep school. "I felt as a good follower of Christ, God had raised me up to do all these things," explains Jeff. "It was way too much." All the doing took a toll on Jeff and his family. Because of all he was doing, Jeff admits that he overlooked his responsibilities to his wife and family.

He realized it was time to do some soul-searching, so he took a sabbatical. Jeff's turning point came when he attended Crossroads Discipleship Training, a program for people who, like him, were in midlife and trying to sort things out. During the program, the work/faith equation became much more integrated.

Jeff attended the program believing his time in the workplace was over, that God was calling him out of business and into a ministry. Unfortunately, he had been led to believe by several people (including pastors) that business was of the world and that as he matured in his faith, Jeff would eventually be led to a higher calling, outside of business. Jeff recalls, "In many ways it left me with a feeling of guilt that as a businessman, I was a second-class Christian."

But Jeff kept searching. After much prayer and discussion with wise people, he discovered that his business was a high calling and that it was his. Jeff Coors was right where God wanted him to be. Says Jeff, "That moment radically changed me. It confirmed to me that business was a legitimate calling equal to any so-called 'ministry.'"

Jeff has found how to integrate his faith and work. He explains, "I am much more into being with God than doing for God. He has given me a real peace about being in the business world, and I have a better understanding of my role. It boils down to being the kind of person God created me to be. I use the Lord's prayer as my guide: 'Thy will be done on earth as it is in heaven.' I believe God has a desire to have His will to be done on earth. Being the person He created me to be will bring Him glory and fulfill His original plan."

Now, instead of changing the world for God, Jeff simply honors his relationship with God and others around him. He understands that God calls us into a relationship first with Him and secondly with the people He has placed around us. Jeff is now President and CEO of Graphic Packaging Corporation and has transformed this simple principle into a very useful and practical tool in business. Graphic Packaging Corporation's Values Statement reflects Jeff's wisdom:

Respect for People

We value each person's intrinsic worth and uniqueness. We acknowledge everyone's contribution and honor his/her opinions. Our work environment is open, honest, supportive, and fulfilling. Our company is built on trust.

Responsibility for Actions and Results

We keep promises. Each person is empowered to make the organization succeed and is 100%

accountable for his/her actions. We challenge the status quo, promote continuous improvement, and reward excellence. We lead by example and do not avoid difficult decisions. We invest in our people and operations for future growth and profit. We work safely, comply with laws, and are a good neighbor. We meet our commitments to share-holders, customers, and employees today and tomorrow.

Relationships with Each Other

Our success is built on quality relationships. We communicate openly and truthfully in a timely manner. We encourage constructive feedback. We are committed to each other and have fun together. We are helpful and compassionate. We treat others the way we want to be treated.

Jeff tells people, "It all boils down to respect and rela-tionships with people. Respecting people is part of who I am. I hold people in ultimate respect, thank them for their contributions, and congratulate them for their successes. Sometimes it is simply being there for them when things don't go well." The values statement has resonated throughout the company. Jeff explains that they started by casually talking about it. Now it is a key foundation of the business.

Today Jeff states he is still a work in progress. He focuses on trying to listen and be a part of God's plan instead of getting out in front of Him. He admits, "I have to fight that all the time. There are still times when I feel that I am not being bold enough. I am not by nature a bold person. During those times of struggle, I make it a point to really stay close to God. However, I can tell you that everything is so much better than before." Through his journey, Jeff has found that he has more peace by working with God than by working for Him.

JOHN D. BECKETT
"Demonstrating Your Faith by Living Your Faith"

John Beckett's newfound relationship with God had created a new life, but it also had created a new dilemma. "How should I relate my faith to my work? Can these two worlds that seem so separate ever merge?" he wondered. For years, John thought that it was most appropriate to follow the rules created by modern culture: Believe in God on Sunday, and get to work on Monday.

John was thrust into the leadership of the family's manufacturing business, R. W. Beckett Corporation, following his father's sudden death. Shortly after, fire nearly consumed the corporation in 1965, yet with tremendous effort, the business survived and even began growing rapidly at a rate of 20 percent per year.

Along with work, which was nearly all-consuming, John and his wife, Wendy, were thoroughly devoted to raising their four children (later to become six). They were growing in their faith and seeing the effect it had on their relationship with family and friends. Yet, John found ever-increasing questions about how to blend his newfound faith with his work.

In John's book, *Loving Monday: Succeeding in Business Without Selling Your Soul,* he describes a defining moment in which he came to the decision that integrating faith and work was the key to running a successful business. He begins by explaining that he had been raised to understand that companies and their employees were better off working in a union-free environment. As a realist, John knew that business leaders could only do so much to influence that decision in their workplace. Under the law, workers are free to form or affiliate with a labor union. But when John thought about a union coming in at R. W. Beckett, he was terrified.

As often happens, the thing he most feared came to pass. John recalls, "When I received the news that an organization attempt was underway, that fear became almost paralyzing in its intensity. Then the fear turned to anger— anger that some of our employees would consider such a course, rather than talk with our management about their concerns."[1]

John decided to enlist the help of a local labor attorney, a man who was known for his tough approach to organization attempts. He agreed to help, but before he had a chance to get very involved, he died of a sudden heart attack. Under increasing pressure, John prayed a heartfelt prayer. "Faced with our attorney's death, I almost concluded we should handle the situation by ourselves," says John. "That was until I happened to be reading from the book of Proverbs, and to my surprise, my eyes fell upon a very pointed verse. In the translation I was reading at the time, Proverbs 12:15 said, 'Don't act without the advice of counsel.' Well, within a few days we had located an attorney from Cleveland who, as it turned out, gave us outstanding advice, helping us guide our month-long campaign to rebuild our employee's confidence in our company."[2]

More than anything, John feared that such a change (unionizing) would destroy the leadership's direct relationship with Beckett's then 30 employees. It seemed clear to John that an outside organization, whose purpose is to stand between employer and employee, could never have the same care and concern for the workers that R. W. Beckett had had over the years. Instead, it most likely would put in a wedge where there had been a close working relationship. John's leadership was solidly based on the biblical model of Ephesians 6 that said employers should conduct themselves with their employees in the same caring and compassionate way that God treats people.

John writes, "So with conviction, good counsel, and a sound strategy, we shared our views and concerns with our employees, all within the tight guidelines imposed by the National Labor Relations Board. A vote was taken, and the overwhelming decision of employees was to stay union-free."[3]

John believes that God helped guide them through that difficult time. But he views it as a big wake-up call, too. "I realized that we had neglected communication," recalls John. "Many aspects of our employee policies and practices were not well understood. Some of our benefits were substandard, and we promptly took steps to improve them."[4]

Such a potential shake-up made John realize that he could not continue living in two separate worlds. It was time to integrate his Sunday beliefs with his Monday through Saturday work week.

Ultimately, John answered three key questions related to incorporating faith and work: (1) How did the R. W. Beckett Corporation, a manufacturer of residential oil burners and related products, successfully integrate faith and work? (2) How was the concept of sharing faith appropriately communicated within a diverse work environment? (3) What have been the consequences of integrating faith and work? The answers to these questions, summarized from John's book, *Loving Monday,* are outlined below.

How did the R. W. Beckett Corporation successfully integrate faith and work?

John's wake-up call made him realize a vital key to the kind of leadership he sought: You can't leave your heart at the door when you come to work. If anything, he realized that compassion and respect are at the very core of a successful business. John backed up his compassion with action, as demonstrated by his following three commitments.

1. Develop the compassionate enterprise; blend accountability and compassion for successful results.

The first truth John realized was that compassion and accountability complement each other. In business, we try to separate the two, and, inevitably, an imbalance occurs, particularly away from compassion and toward accountability. As John sees it, "Compassion without accountability produces sentimentalism. Accountability without compassion is harsh and heartless. Compassion teamed up with accountability is a powerful force—one which we have found can provide a great incentive to excel."[5]

John provides several examples of how the combination of compassion and accountability benefit the R. W. Beckett Corporation:

- When a person is passed over for a promotion, management will follow up, show appreciation for his or her stepping forward, and then point out how he or she can strengthen his/her qualifications. Management will then encourage the person to apply for advancement in the future.
- When a customer has had a reversal and needs an extension of credit, the company is

mindful of the risk but is also understanding, going the extra mile to be of help when it is wise to do so.

- When an employee is going to be terminated, the company provides the employee with as much dignity and compassion as possible. John explains, "First, we go through whatever process is necessary to make a firm decision. This is an analytical step, dealing squarely with reality. The second is the termination itself, which should be carried out with all the compassion we can muster. An effort should be made to cushion the transition, such as a severance arrangement and possibly the use of outplacement services. But the key is to see the process as redemptive, a step which God can use to accomplish His larger purposes in the person's life and in the organization."[6]

2. Be committed to employee growth and development; create blueprints for success.

At the core of John's compassion for others lies a passion and belief that every employee has an ability to successfully fulfill his or her God-given destiny. "I feel we are at our highest and best as an employer if we can provide a context for growth and enable our employees to find and fit in with God's blueprint for their lives."[7]

3. Encourage employees to be committed to their families and to prioritize family over work.

John recognizes that the work/family balance issue is one of the most critical issues facing businesses today. He knows that the choices between work and family can be difficult to make, especially as the demands of work grow due to downsizing, which places heavier burdens on those who survive the cuts.

Recognizing the difficulty of this dilemma, John made a major commitment to prioritize family over work. "Our priorities should be ordered like this: First, our relationship with God; then commitment to family; and then commitment to our work and vocations."[8] The R. W. Beckett Corporation backed up these beliefs with these family-oriented policies:

- **Maternity Leave:** The company gives the employee an opportunity to stay at home for up to 26 weeks. During this period, the employee maintains his or her income at one-quarter the normal level. The company will loan the employee an additional one quarter, providing up to half of his or her normal wages. For up to three years after the birth of a child, the employee has the option of returning to work part-time, sharing his or her job with another employee, or doing work at home. The latter two options depend on availability.

- **Adoption:** The company provides a $1,000 adoption benefit and, in certain cases, has provided paid time off where travel to a foreign destination is necessary to complete the adoption.

- **Travel Policies:** The company tries to limit the nights employees must be away from home. R. W. Beckett does not insist, as some do, that employees travel over Saturdays to take advantage of reduced fares.

- **Open Houses and Company Visits:** Management recognizes that most young children have no idea what job their parents do during the day. They simply see Mom or Dad disappearing and reappearing on a daily basis. The company has open houses and company visits in which children are invited to visit on a special day so parents can show the children where, how, and with whom they work.

- **Company Newsletters:** The company provides family-oriented newsletters, mailed to employees' homes, with human interest stories to help build bridges between work and family.

- **Hiring Family and Relatives:** The company recognizes the risks of hiring relatives but also sees the rewards. The company maintains safe-guards such as not allowing family members to report to each other and overall has found the policy beneficial to both the family and the organization.

How was the concept of sharing faith appropriately communicated within a diverse work environment?

These written statements are communicated to all stakeholders of the R. W. Beckett Corporation:

Vision
Our vision is to build a family of companies, each of which serves its customers in distinctive and impor-tant ways, and each of which reflects the practical application of biblical values throughout.

Guiding Principles
Focus: We are a Christ-centered company.

People: We build and maintain solid relationships of respect among ourselves, our customers, and our suppliers, encouraging the growth and well-being of each employee.

Conduct: We will conduct ourselves with dignity, adhering to the highest ethical and moral standards.

Work environment: We aspire to be a great place to work: a progressive, dynamic, and continuously improving company that embraces world-class practices in quality, timing, involvement, and simplicity.

Stewardship: Our business is a trust, and we will be good stewards of every resource in our care.

Citizenship: We want to serve others, helping meet human needs in the community and beyond.

John justifies the forthright reference to being a Christ-centered, biblically based company, something that happened quite naturally because of the company's basic values. No one imposed these values; rather they evolved from the process of the company defining itself. When a company's values and the bottom-line clash, priorities get reevaluated. John explains, "As we point out in explaining our vision to employees, every enterprise is guided by *some* point of view, some undergirding philosophy. Our management has elected to have biblical tenets and principles serve as that guide."[9]

Of course, employees don't have to agree. John continues, "We are careful to be inclusive of any employee's faith, making sure religious beliefs have no bearing on his or her opportunity to work with or advance in our companies; rather we seek to view all with equal appreciation and respect."[10]

What have been the consequences of integrating faith and work?

It has now been over twenty-five years since the union situation changed John's view about integrating faith into his work. The consequences of integrating the two have been twofold: financial and interpersonal.

Financially, the R. W. Beckett Corporation has grown from a small, unknown company with $4 million in revenue to a nationally known company which, with its affiliates, has revenues of approximately $100 million. In terms of market share, the company has grown from a company with minimal marketplace recognition to commanding 75 percent of the North American market.

John is excited when he talks about the impact incorporating faith and work has on people. "I can honestly say that I have never been challenged on any level, from employees, management, our board, our customers, or our suppliers regarding this issue," he says. "We are constantly surveying our employees, vendors, and customers for their feedback. The response has been consistent. They view us as people of integrity. We are people who are consistent and can be counted on."

John has learned that incorporating faith and work does not force one person's will over another's. In fact, it provides the opposite; it provides freedom for individuals to fulfill their destiny in the workplace.

John's message to others is one of true appreciation. "In America, we are very privileged to have the freedom to integrate our faith and our work," says John. "I find each day is important and filled with opportunity—not just to 'survive the rat race,' but to actually have a part, however small, in consciously knitting what I do into God's larger purposes. If I can do that in a way that serves the Lord and brings glory to Him, as well as blessing our employees and business associates, I will have considered my work to be of great value."[11]

CONCLUSION

Integrating work and faith is about bringing who we are to work. Each of us is completely free to be a godly leader at work. No one can separate us from our faith. Still, we wonder, "Who am I at work?" "Do my actions, behaviors, decisions, and speech reflect God's nature?" Many of us feel we have to work for God like we work for our boss. We need to do something, achieve something, change something. Maybe, as Jeff Coors learned, we are called to simply be with Him.

Jeff Coors, John Beckett, and other successful leaders follow three principles when integrating their faith and work:

1. Leadership by Example

In Matthew 5:16, Jesus said that we were to be salt and light. In essence, we are to reflect

God's nature for others to see. We reflect God's nature in our business decisions, our relationships with our employees and customers, and our behaviors. There is no easy or pre-formulated three-step process to successfully integrating faith and work. It is an everyday process of walking with God. We are constantly bombarded with decisions: Should I remain quiet if there is an opportunity to speak up? Should I listen instead of speak? Should I share with someone in need?

Ralph Waldo Emerson said, "Who you are speaks so loudly I can hardly hear what you are saying." Simply put, we can relax, focus on our relationship with God, and allow His presence to shine through us.

2. Respect

A common principle followed by Jeff Coors, John Beckett, and other leaders I interviewed was respect for others. Each leader had a strong belief that every individual should be treated with respect and dignity. Respect honors diversity and others' rights. Respect for others comes from the heart. It is not a program we must follow; it's part of our nature as godly leaders.

The simplest guide is to follow the golden rule, Matthew 7:12, "Do to others what you would have them do to you." I know of a large

Minnesota-based multinational company whose business is primarily based in Southeast Asia. The differences in culture and religion resulted in difficulties agreeing on major business issues. This company found that using the golden rule helped establish a foundation of mutual respect that led to open communication and meaningful working relationships.

3. Compassion

John Beckett showed us that love plays an important role in business. At the R. W. Beckett Company, showing compassion for employees, customers, and vendors is part of their business. When it comes to bringing our faith to work, no organization and no person can stop us from loving others and showing compassion for a fellow worker. No one can prevent us from praying for another person. No one can prevent us from being who we are except ourselves. In I Corinthians 13 we are reminded that "love is patient, kind, is not self-seeking, does not envy, does not easily anger and always trusts, always hopes, and always perseveres." Our workplaces are desperately looking for people to express that kind of love. We can do that every single day without ever asking permission or forming a special interest committee to look into the matter and develop a plan.

We've seen the challenges and opportunities of integrating faith and work. We all come from unique backgrounds and have diverse viewpoints. We all work in vastly different situations, but we all can integrate our faith and work. First and foremost, we must have the courage to be who we are as godly people. Nothing speaks louder. As for a specific dilemma we may have at work, we can prayerfully bring the issue to God and others. Questions like the ones that follow will help clarify the situation and bring us ideas for how to proceed.

DISCUSSION GUIDE

1. Do you feel free to demonstrate your faith at work? Describe your comfort level as it relates to being who you are (mentally and spiritually) at work.
2. What keeps you from expressing your faith at work?
3. Specifically describe the boundaries you feel are appropriate as they relate to integrating your faith and work.
4. What do you feel is God's will for you in the integration of your faith and work?
5. What specific action steps will you take to find more peace and fulfillment in the integration of your faith with your work?

Notes

1. John D. Beckett, *Loving Monday: Succeeding in Business Without Selling Your Soul* (Downers Grove, IL: InterVarsity Press, 1998), 55. Used with permission.
2. Ibid, 56.
3. Ibid, 57.
4. Ibid, 57.
5. Ibid, 110.
6. Ibid, 111–112.
7. Ibid, 95.
8. Ibid, 130.
9. Ibid, 146.
10. Ibid, 146.
11. Ibid, 170.

Yielding Control

From "surrender means defeat"
to "surrender means victory"

For whoever wants to save his life will lose it,
but whoever loses his life for me will find it.
What good will it be for a man if he gains the
whole world, yet forfeits his soul?

—Matthew 16:25

Issue: How do I deal with circumstances that are beyond my control?

I facilitated a strategic planning session for a small, rapidly growing health care organization. They were experiencing significant change in their marketplace. The changes were fast and powerful, and they had to be dealt with swiftly or the company would go under. In a meeting, we identified all the changes and came up with good strategies to address them. The executive team was apprehensive, but overall they were unified about the changes the organization had to make.

But not Jan, the Vice President of Operations. She resisted every single new strategy and had an argument for every change that needed to take place. In essence, she was the biggest control freak on the team. The greater the uncertainty, the greater her resistance. Unfortunately, Jan became a major stumbling block in the strategic planning process. The true tragedy was that Jan was extremely talented and capable, yet she was quickly becoming a liability to the organization. She desperately tried to control the circumstances surrounding her as the riptide of change swept her away. The executive team had to respond quickly to the changes that were occurring, and cooperation from Jan's position was critical to their success. As a result, they had to replace Jan.

Jan's situation brings up a challenging question. When is it time to take charge and when is it time to relinquish control?

Solution: Do my part, and let God do His.

Every day, many business leaders try to control situations that they have no control over. The harder they flex their muscles, the more they lose control. Generally, the greater a leader's power, the harder it is for him or her to relinquish control to a higher authority. Many leaders call on God like they call on a consultant, to help them with their problems. They may go as far as delegating some control, but in no way will they relinquish total control.

In this chapter, we will learn about two leaders who were faced with turbulent conditions. Tad Piper, Chairman and CEO of Piper Jaffray Companies, Inc., an investment management firm, tells his story of surrendering control and power. Jim Secord, President and CEO of Lakewood Publications, publisher of *Training* magazine and various books and newsletters, shares his story about cooperating with circumstances. In both, we learn that surrendering control to God is a better plan than trying to take charge of things beyond our control.

TAD PIPER
"Relinquishing Control"

Tad Piper, Chairman and CEO of Piper Jaffray Companies, Inc., typified the high-powered executive. Like many executives, he was a take-charge person who made things happen. Tad was the third-generation Piper to lead the highly respected investment firm that enjoyed a 100-year tradition of excellence, service, and integrity. He enjoyed all the trappings that came with the position: wealth, community standing, and power. Executives like Tad have a powerful need to be in control of the circumstances that surround them. Tad believed that with his power and influence, nothing was beyond his control, until one day in April 1994, the bleakest day in his life.

That was the day the most respected financial newspaper in the world, the *Wall Street Journal,* proclaimed Piper Jaffray bankrupt. The *Journal* reported that Piper Jaffray's fixed income portfolio manager had begun using borrowed money to amplify returns and had invested in derivatives—hybrid investments developed to boost yields at a time when bond prices were soaring and yields were crashing—which exposed investors to a higher degree of risk than expected. After six interest rate increases in 10 months, the bond and derivative markets crashed. Investors in Piper Jaffray's bond fund, many of whom had enjoyed spectacular returns in these funds, saw the market value of these funds drop over $.5 billion.

The effects were felt around the world. Pension funds declared disastrous results on their balance sheets. Individual investors were furious. The *Wall Street Journal* claimed Piper Jaffray's liabilities exceeded their assets and that they didn't have the means to reimburse their customers for the losses. Tad attempted to respond to the article and put the truth in context, but it was too late. Reporters, lawyers, and government regulators burst through the doors of the Piper Jaffray institution with the intensity of a raging firestorm. Tad quickly found himself in unfamiliar territory. He was in the world spotlight, and he had experienced a blow that brought him to his knees.

"I felt terrible," Tad recalls. "Here we had a 100-year-old company whose mission was to serve our clients and not disappoint them, and I felt we had let them down. I also felt betrayed by the people I trusted. I just couldn't believe this was happening. I repeated over and over, 'What did I ever do to deserve this? Why me?'"

The enormous personal burden Tad felt became all-consuming. He explains, "I had to figure this thing out because the potential consequence of not sorting it out was staggering. My reaction was 'Well, so be it. I will roll up my sleeves and dig us out of this mess. I'll get the press straightened out, I'll fight the lawyers, I'll visit every unhappy customer, I'll fly to every branch office to explain the situation and console every angry employee, and I'll fix the market.'"

As valiant as Tad's efforts were, no matter what he did, he could not quell the firestorm. Relentless pressure came from every angle. Day after day, Tad dealt with the problem and its consequences: class-action suits, a vicious press, unhappy clients, and government regulators. The same questions pounded on Tad: "Were you at fault?" "Did you make false promises?" "Did you falsely advertise?" "Are you going out of business?" The pressure grew worse with each passing day, and underneath the surface, Tad was crumbling.

After four months in a focused "I can fix it" mode, Tad had neared the end of his rope. A sense of desperation crept in. There was no light at the end of this tunnel, only darkness. His earlier thoughts ran through his mind. "I just gotta get this right. There is too much riding on this to screw it up! I must handle it! I am not a quitter!" In the middle of this battle, Tad saw only problems. He was no longer fighting the lawyers and the media; the battle was in his own mind, and he was losing.

Then one day Tad received a package from an employee who himself had gone through a painful situation. The small package contained a tape recording of a sermon along with a brief note that read: "Heard this, it helped me, maybe it can help you. God bless." Tad appreciated the gift from a caring friend and slipped the tape in his briefcase.

Two weeks later, Tad remembered the tape and popped it into his cassette player. The sermon, on the story of Job, got his attention because he could relate to Job. Intellectually, Tad knew that God was and is the center of the universe; Tad wasn't. He had learned that lesson two years earlier when he had admitted he was an alcoholic. Although rereading the Alcoholics Anonymous *Big Book* and the Book of Job helped Tad cope temporarily, he was still not at peace. He simply could not relax until he fixed this thing. Too much was at stake.

A few weeks later, Tad reached his breaking point. It wasn't any one particular incident; it was sheer exhaustion that did him in. Completely overwhelmed, he couldn't go on. "I remember lying awake in my bed, yet another sleepless night, in total despair, thinking, 'Oh my God! I just can't handle it any more. It's just not possible. I can't do it. It's not possible. It's just too much!' At some point I remember praying, 'Lord, I just can't do it, so you have to!' All of a sudden, I remembered, 'Wait a minute, I'm not alone. I don't have to do it alone. There is help.'" Relief flooded through the broken man. He had finally reached the place where he knew God was in control and Tad was not. Tad's crisis was over. The crisis was not just about the circumstance he was in; it was also about his need to surrender to God.

Life was different after that night. Tad was at peace, and it showed. Slowly, Tad's world began to change. "Because I knew God was with me all the time," says Tad,

"I was able to navigate through some pretty troubled waters while keeping myself on an even keel. I worked just as hard, but it was much easier with my Partner (with the big P) with me. I was calmer. I became more rational about what I was capable of doing. I allowed others around me to do their jobs. The calm that was in me allowed others to be calm."

His relationships improved overall, but Tad's relationship with his lawyers improved most. Although they were all on the same side, Tad had been in constant conflict with them. The lawyers were looking out for the company's best interests, and Tad was looking out for the clients' best interests. Those differing viewpoints created stress. When Tad relaxed, he started to see a bigger picture solution. His calmer demeanor allowed for better communication to develop between him and his lawyers. They eventually started to work together in harmony.

In addition to being more at peace, Tad opened up. Before, Tad felt he had to be strong for others. He could not and would not show his vulnerability to others because that would be a sign of weakness. Tad realized that his surrender to God was not defeat, but was victory over the circumstances he had tried to control. Not being in control was actually liberating! It was no longer about hiding his weakness, but about sharing in God's strength.

Tad discovered that communicating his true vulnerable self was much more of a blessing to others than trying to be strong for them. Tad recalled the time he and his wife Cindy openly shared their pain to all the spouses at the Piper

Jaffray National Managers' Meeting. Tad explains, "The ordeal took its toll on everyone in the company. We recognized that everyone was affected, particularly the spouses. Many employees thought we were the king and queen. We wanted to show them that we were just like them—real people in real pain." He and Cindy didn't make any speeches; they just talked, sharing everything from Tad's alcoholism to their faith. Their openness had a major effect on the company's employees. The Pipers' vulnerability gave the employees permission to be vulnerable, too. And that became a turning point for the organization.

Tad recalls, "When I was an alcoholic, I typically retreated to a lonely place, and lonely was not a good place to be. Two years later when the bond fiasco hit, I felt alone with a huge burden that I had to fix. Today, I realize that I was never alone. The Lord was with me as an alcoholic and He was with me through this long ordeal." Tad realizes that if he were still a practicing alcoholic when this recent ordeal occurred, it would have been all over for him and the Piper Jaffray Companies, Inc.

Looking back, Tad says he can see clearly how God was with him. All along Tad was surrounded by people who cared, even though at the time he couldn't see it. His wife Cindy lovingly stood by him through both ordeals, and his friends and associates were there for him, too. Says Tad, "My advice to others is to listen to those who love you. Take a risk, be vulnerable, find a place to go to help you deal with the loneliness."

In 1999, Tad gave a speech to 300 corporate executives in Minneapolis. In his closing remarks, he spoke openly about his ordeal. "My Partner (with the big P) and I work well together, at least when I am paying attention. I find myself looking for joy in every single day and feel able to find it, and feel blessed to be part of His world. I would like to close with a familiar prayer: 'God grant me the serenity to accept the things I cannot change, the courage to change the things I can, and the wisdom to know the difference.' Thy will, not mine, be done."

How did this chapter in Tad's life end? Not only did Piper Jaffray survive, they thrived. Rising from the depths of destruction, they are now a highly successful $800-million company and in 1998 were sold to a large regional financial services firm.

It's no coincidence that Tad's turning point came in the dark of night, while lying in bed. Flat on his back, he no longer saw the storm of problems that surrounded him. Instead, he had the privilege of looking up and seeing that God was with him in the storm. Tad may have lost sight of God in the midst of his problems, but God never lost sight of Tad. He was never alone.

JIM SECORD
"Cooperating with Uncertainty"

Jim Secord is no stranger to change. As President and CEO of Lakewood Publications (now a division of Bill Communications) and recent winner of the Hedley Donovan Award for his contributions to the magazine industry, he steered his organization through the turbulence of being sold three times in less than 16 months. Lakewood Publications flourished, immediately experiencing two of the most profitable years in the company's history in 1994 and 1995.

It was up to Jim to help Lakewood's employees deal with the trauma of uncertainty. He knew that significant change always takes its toll and can be exhausting. And he was not immune to its effect, either.

Jim had learned all about that in 1979, the year Lakewood had a significant layoff. Unfortunately, it was handled poorly. There wasn't much compassion shown in cutting jobs. This created bad feelings for Lakewood's employees, ranging from anger to anxiety. For Jim, not being in control of the circumstances resulted in tremendous stress. He recalls, "I was president at the time and I ended up in the hospital with acute pericarditis. I thought I was having heart attack. I remember going to the CEO and stating, 'This will never happen again. It's too painful for everyone.'" Because of that time, Jim changed the way he deals with uncertainty and relates to people. He decided that the best way is to help people through change, creating as little trauma and pain as possible.

Jim's lesson taught him not to resist the unknown of change, but to manage it with courage and compassion. He explains that even though the pain cannot always be avoided, it can be managed so a company doesn't lose its most important asset: a committed staff.

Jim identified four principles that helped Lakewood's 100 employees remain focused and committed during this 16-month period of change:

1. A Shared Vision of Success Based on Shared Values

Since 1994, Lakewood has had a vision statement in place that underscores trust, integrity, dignity, and open communication. It was hammered out over a two-year period, during which all 100 employees were asked to participate. More than 450 inputs were gathered through interviews, questionnaires, and the use of an organizational development consultant. "We argued things through and reexamined the company," Jim explains. "The shared vision was the glue that kept us together during the turbulence—it was our benchmark, our guidepost, and a piece of hope."

2. Open Communication

"Open communication was the antidote to crippling change," declares Jim. "In those 16 months, even though we were deeply involved in the transactions, we managed to hold six company-wide meetings and we 'memoed' people to death, just to reassure them and keep them posted." Because of the air of uncertainty, Jim made it a point to walk the floor as much as possible, sitting on the corners of people's desks and asking, "What questions do you have? Let me hear what's on your mind."

Nothing was held back. Even the financial information and selling presentation were made available to the employees, the same as was given to potential buyers. Jim recalls, "Communication is a conscious act. It was also a part of who we were as a culture. It was important not only to communicate with them honestly, but also to ask how they were feeling and let them express their fears, so we could address their concerns."

3. Personal Integrity

"As leaders, we are the role models—that's our charge," says Jim. "The associates looked to me to see how I behaved in difficult circumstances. That's where the trust comes in."

Personal integrity builds trust. During the third sale, the new company offered Jim a "stay bonus" of $75,000 for continuing with the company through the transition. Instead, Jim decided to share his bonus equally with all the full-time employees who stayed through the sale. "My philosophy was that we were all in this together, so the decision was easy. It was the right thing to do."

4. Preparation for Gut-Wrenching Change

At a meeting in New York with Lakewood's new owners, Jim heard the words he most dreaded. "Jim, we are not going to be able to keep the financial department." He winced as he thought of letting 12 loyal employees go. As painful as it was, he knew he had to conduct the process with as much dignity and respect as possible.

Jim's pain is still evident as he tells of that experience. "The most difficult time I can recall was when I needed to get in front of my associates after they stuck with the mission and tell them it was necessary to cut 12 people," he recalls. "I knew they would be upset, but I remember preparing them for change and that this was one of the unfortunate realities of change. I told them that it was okay to be angry, to grieve, and that we would help them work through it. I told them we would do whatever we could to help them transition to other jobs. Looking back at that time, everything turned out very well. No one ever came back to us and said that we lied to them or didn't tell them the truth."

As Jim and I were wrapping up our discussion, a conversation ensued that showed how prophetic his final comments about preparing for gut-wrenching change really were. As we prepared to end the interview, I glanced at a beautiful bouquet of flowers on Jim's desk. "Where did you get the flowers?" I asked. Jim smiled as he explained, "Oh, they're from my wife, D'Arcy. She always does things like that." Jim then shared with me that D'Arcy, at the age of 58, is battling Alzheimer's disease.

"In everyone's life we come to forks in the road. It's not something we want, but it's there. We're then faced with decisions. I could get the best care for D'Arcy and go on with my job. Instead, I have elected to leave the company to be with her. I want to be in a new relationship with her; a new way to love. I haven't figured all the ways to do that, but I will do it and we will walk this journey together. D'Arcy may not understand the same kind of journey when I communicate with her. I may not be speaking to her cognitive mind, but I will be talking to her spiritually. I really believe that God has a purpose in this. D'Arcy is giving to me and to others in her own special way and I am trying to find out what that is. Also, this is my opportunity to give in a whole new way."

Even though Jim has been with the company for 37 years, he says the decision to leave was easy. "I see this situation as a pretty amazing gift," he says. "Once again, I find myself facing uncertainty. In the case of D'Arcy, this situation is much more uncertain than the trauma of the three changes in company ownership. I always felt we would pull through and have a positive outcome with the company changes. With D'Arcy, I feel like I am going into completely uncharted waters. It's extremely tough, yet I firmly believe this will turn into a potentially magnificent journey."

Conclusion

Each leader reaches a point in his or her life where he or she has to ask, "Who's in charge here?" Harry Truman coined the phrase, "The buck stops here," implying that the leader is the one in control, the one with the final responsibility. However, Tad and Jim show us that though leaders are responsible for and accountable to do the things in their power, they are not responsible for, nor can they control, certain outcomes. No matter how powerful a leader is, there are some things a person has absolutely no control over. This is a very difficult message for most leaders to grasp, as the corporate world supports a leader who is in control and in charge. In the business world, surrender is associated with defeat. In the spiritual realm, however, relinquishing control to God's plan is victory.

To understand why surrender means victory, we need to define surrender. The dictionary gives two distinct definitions. One definition is to give up or to quit; the other is to yield to another's power. The kind of surrender we are speaking of doesn't mean quitting or giving up. It does mean yielding our need to be in control to a much higher authority. Surrender provides us with victory because we are free from the anguish, fear, and guilt that is associated with trying to hold on to something we have no control over. It means we will be at peace, knowing that God is ultimately in charge.

Tad Piper had to come to a place where he could admit he simply couldn't handle the burden of his problem anymore. He finally admitted he was not in control. He started to live again the moment he realized he was not alone, when he turned to God and said, "Lord, I can't do it, so you have to."

Jim Secord is moving into the most uncertain time in his life. He admitted that it is extremely tough to deal with his wife's Alzheimer's, yet he approaches the experience as a "potentially magnificent journey." He cooperates with uncertainty, not knowing the outcome, but knowing that God is in charge of the situation.

When we are challenged by a need for control, we can choose to view our relationship with God as a partnership rather than as one of a boss and subordinate. Our goal is to walk with God one moment, one day, at a time. Dale Carnegie gave a great suggestion to live in "day-tight compartments." Quite simply, we have no control over yesterday and no control of tomorrow. We can only do those things that are within our control today. When we wake up in the morning, we can review the most important issues we have pressing for that day. Then we prioritize and divide these responsibilities into two categories: things within my control that I will do today, and things outside my control that I will give to God today. Finally, we just work all the things that are within our authority to do.

If we live the day knowing God has a plan for our lives and is in control of all our circumstances, we can learn to cooperate with the uncertainty of a sale, job promotion, or other change by performing the tasks we have in front of us. The uncertainty cannot rob us of the importance of the moment.

DISCUSSION GUIDE

1. What specifically is out of your control, yet causes you worry?
2. What are the things within your control that you can do today?
3. What things can you relinquish and put in God's hands?
4. What things can you do to cooperate with uncertainty?

7

Tough Decisions

From giving into
discouragement
to living with hope

*Blessed is the man who finds wisdom, the man who
gains understanding, for she is more profitable than
silver and yields better returns than gold.*

–Proverbs 3:13–14

Issue: What do I do when faced with choosing between a bad solution and a worse solution?

I remember having breakfast with a good friend, John, who was in the midst of a lose-lose dilemma. Faced with one of the biggest decisions of his life, he was mentally exhausted and discouraged. As he described his dilemma to me, John sketched the pros and cons of each decision on his paper napkin. He and his family would experience significant pain regardless of his decision. After 45 minutes, he realized he was talking in circles and finding no solution. Silently, he stared at the notes he had scribbled and mindlessly began doodling on the napkin. John then drew a big horseshoe around the notes and moaned, "If I could just go around this issue."

Have you been in a situation that appeared hopeless? Or have you been in a lose-lose dilemma where a positive resolution seemed impossible? There are times when there is no way around our dilemmas; we can only go through them. We have to go through our issue in order to make the best decision.

Solution: Seek God's wisdom to turn a bad problem into a good solution.

One of the greatest flaws of many of today's leaders is their avoidance of making tough decisions. While courage is doing the right thing, wisdom is knowing the right thing to do. Hope is the confident expectation of God's solution, even though you can't see the answer in front of you. Effective leaders seek God's wisdom in their present circumstances and live with hope that God will reveal the right, and best, solution.

Two leaders who appeared to be in lose-lose circumstances shared their win-win solutions with me. Linda Rios Brook, former President and General Manager of KLGT-TV in Minneapolis/St. Paul, helped turn a lose-lose decision into a significant win. Brenda Scott, CEO of the Mobile, Alabama Convention and Visitors Commission, proved that seeking God's wisdom and having hope can transform a divisive community. Her leadership helped a city overcome its past difficulties and find new hope for the future. Both leaders found that God provides unexpected solutions to those who do not give up hope.

LINDA RIOS BROOK
"Discovering the Win in a Lose-Lose Situation"

Linda Rios Brook, then President and General Manager of KLGT-TV in Minneapolis/St. Paul, was facing a very difficult dilemma: Should she keep her highest rated and most profitable program, "The Jerry Springer Show," or should she not renew? As President and General Manager, she had a financial obligation to provide a good return on investment to her shareholders. On the other hand, "The Jerry Springer Show" provided little value to her family-friendly audience. If she had been pressured by outside forces, making one decision or another would have been easier. Unfortunately, the easy way out never happened, and the ultimate decision-making responsibility was placed squarely on her shoulders.

Right up front, Linda admits that she had a love/hate relationship with "The Jerry Springer Show." "I loved the revenue and ratings," she says, "and absolutely hated the show." It was up to her to preview every show, and regularly, at least one to two times a week, Linda would send a show back to the producers because of the content. She saw that as time went on, the shows were getting progressively worse. "When the contract was coming up for

138

renewal, I was leaning toward not renewing the contract," explains Linda.

The show's producers learned Linda was thinking of not renewing and were concerned. They knew the show had the highest rating in the marketplace, so keeping the contract was a big priority. In situations like this, the producers bring in a show's star to close the deal. They arranged to have Linda meet with Jerry Springer at a convention in Las Vegas.

Linda chuckles as she remembers her meeting with Jerry Springer. "I spoke candidly about my concerns for the show," she recalls. "He said his show was actually a morality play where good triumphs over evil. As we discussed the issue further, he stood up and claimed, 'I will stand before God and be able to defend what I have done!' I remember thinking 'I'm going to move back a bit in case lightning strikes him!'"

Linda decided to renew the contract with Springer. "Life is much more complex than making a good decision or bad decision," she explains. "Sometimes you don't have an option between a good decision and bad decision. The only option is between a bad decision and a worse decision. That's much harder because you don't have fans, only critics, on both sides of the argument." Linda believes that her first priority is to do the very best she can for the people she works for. Therefore, she felt her primary obligation was to fulfill her role as President and General Manager. "I had to remember what my job was," she says. "And my job was to run the television station as a business. That meant competing in the market, growing the audience, and providing a good return on investment to my shareholders."

But even after reminding herself of all that, Linda wasn't at peace with her decision. She explains, "I knew people would disagree with my rationale and decision, but that wasn't what bothered me. It was most important to be accountable to God. I believe spiritual maturity is when the Lord brings you to a point where you are only accountable to Him. There is no one to blame your decision on. After I made my decision, I spent a good deal of time worrying about "The Springer Show" and the negative effect it had on people. I knew this was not what I was in television for."

Linda continued to struggle with her decision. She asked herself two key questions: "Is there anything redeeming about this dilemma? Is there any redemption in the sleaze? Linda tells about the day she was in her monthly prayer meeting, thinking to herself, "Why do people watch Jerry Springer?" Then she realized that people who stay up late at night watching Springer are people who want to see a life that's worse than their own. She could only assume that the show somehow helped them cope with their own dismal situations. "If that was true," Linda considered, "then the people watching Springer must have a lot of problems."

After much thought and prayer, Linda came up with a third option, one that transcended the either/or dilemma she had struggled with. Linda remembered a friend who ran a biblically principled crisis counseling center in the area. Dan's counseling center provided help for all kinds of people who were hurting. She approached Dan with her idea, saying, "How would you like to try an experiment? What if we put a crawl, like the weather warnings across the bottom of the TV screen, which says 'NEED A FRIEND?' with the number of your crisis counseling service?" Dan agreed to the experiment.

The first night they were flooded with hundreds of calls, literally jamming their phone lines. Over the next three years, "The Jerry Springer Show" produced thousands of phone calls. The calls ranged from the serious to the outrageous. Some callers thought it was a phone sex line. Some calls were from pranksters. But the majority of callers were hurting and in serious trouble. Clearly, the crawl across the bottom of the TV screen had a profound effect on a lot of people.

The counseling center's executive director theorized that, thanks to Jerry Springer, hundreds of hurting people began a personal relationship with God. One of the crisis counselors, Paul, shared some of the most bizarre stories of people who had called to pull a prank or to have phone sex only to have their lives transformed by God. The typical caller was a young person between the ages of 14 and 25. He described one that typified many of their calls.

"I received a call from a group of three or four teenage girls who called as a prank," Paul says. "One girl was on the phone, and I could hear the other girls laughing in the background. At first, the caller was mocking me as the others snickered in the background. As time passed, the girl began to share what appeared to be true facts about her life. She talked about her mom and her 'jerk boyfriend.' When the caller started to become serious, I heard the other girls start to mock her. Even when the other girls harassed the caller, she continued to talk. Eventually she went upstairs to get away from her friends and called me from the upstairs bathroom. She asked tons of questions, and I could hear her soften. A week later she called again and asked a bunch more questions." Two years later, Paul received a letter from that girl thanking him for helping her get out of an impossible situation.

What had Paul learned from this Jerry Springer experience? As a former alcohol and drug abuser himself, Paul was a street-wise young man who thought he had seen it all. These callers, from sex perverts to people who would get on the phone and cry, took Paul on a wild ride. Each caller seemed so lost or angry that Paul didn't see how he could possibly help them. After three years, he is convinced that God can do anything, even when it appears the situation is hopeless. Paul explains, "This experience taught me that no situation is impossible. I will never quit on anyone or anything."

This story shows us how God works through people in order to accomplish His plan. Linda Rios Brook was confronted with what appeared to be a lose-lose decision, yet she never quit or opted for an easy solution. Though she didn't immediately have an answer, she defined what was important and what her role in the solution was, and she worked diligently toward a positive solution. Linda comments, "Oftentimes, you don't have perfect elements to work with. Within those imperfect ones, you need to ask yourself, 'Is there a way to do my job and still be faithful to the things that are really important to God?'"

Linda maintained accountability to solve her dilemma. While she didn't see the answer directly in front of her, she believed that with God anything is possible. She didn't use God to solve her problems; God used her to create solutions. God is creative, and He sends creative solutions. Linda's role was not to solve this particular problem; her role was to be available and accountable in the midst of the dilemma.

Brenda J. Scott
"Finding Hope in a Hopeless Situation"

One the most frustrating and painful strategic planning retreats I have ever facilitated was with the all-male board of directors of the Mobile Convention and Visitors' Corporation in Mobile, Alabama, that had a long history of racial tension. Half of the board members, including the chairman, were African-American; the other half, including the CEO, were Caucasian. Upon my arrival, I learned they were embroiled in a bitter issue involving a racial incident within the organization. The incident inflamed an already tense situation, resulting in the firing of the CEO and a deep rift in the organization, with stakeholders firmly planted on both sides of the situation. To complicate it further, the local media became actively involved, heightening tension and leaving the entire community both frustrated and mistrusting.

We had just ended the all-day session in which significant progress had been made. The board members had spoken honestly regarding how to resolve the racial incident, then came to consensus and developed a solid strategy to move forward. Around the table, board members were packing up their briefcases and shaking hands. As one of the board members opened the door to leave, a reporter and cameraman burst through the doors and ran up to the chairman. The cameraman turned the bright lights on, shining them into the chairman's eyes while the reporter shoved a microphone toward his face. Within moments, the reporter bombarded the chairman with misleading and inflammatory questions. Ill-prepared, the chairman sputtered and reeled from the reporter's assault. He tried to share the truth, but it was twisted around by the series of questions. The positive progress that had been made over several hours was thrown out the door in less than a minute. The chairman's unintentional response to the reporter exacerbated the situation, making a bad situation worse.

I remember flying home feeling angry and frustrated. "This situation is impossible," I said to myself. "There are too many obstacles for this to improve." I was skeptical that anything or anyone could break down the walls of mistrust in that city. As I watched the sunset through my window on the plane, I sadly and reluctantly gave up and turned my thoughts to my next assignment.

Two years after that frustrating strategic planning retreat in Mobile, Alabama, I bumped into an African-American woman named Brenda Scott at a Seattle convention. Her name badge caught my eye: Her title was CEO of that very same convention bureau. Considering the city's past, I was somewhat taken aback that its new CEO was both African-American and female.

I introduced myself, cautiously told her that I had worked with her organization two years ago, and asked her to describe its current status. Brenda proceeded to tell me how great things were and how their business was growing by leaps and bounds. She continued on with stories of teamwork, community support, and economic growth. I couldn't believe it. Was this really the same city? Finally, I asked her point blank, "In the midst of racial tension, an all-male board, mistrust, and skepticism, how did you turn around such a seemingly hopeless situation?" Her response: "God."

From there, Brenda shared the story of how she walked in God's wisdom, from her first employment interview to the organization's current success, all in a mere two years.

Brenda told me that from the beginning, she sought God's wisdom. "I prayed—first for the wisdom to move through the confusion and misunderstandings, then for protection from the adversaries who wanted to see me fail. I knew how difficult this job was going to be. I prayed for guidance regarding whether to take this job and felt that God called me to this city for a reason." Then Brenda described how God helped her establish her credibility and rebuild trust with each stakeholder group, first with the board, then with her staff, and eventually with the community.

Her first step was the interview process. From the start, Brenda boldly communicated who she was. On her resume, she wrote that she was "God-based, heart-led, and people-motivated." She reiterated this approach during her interview with the selection committee. "I remember the selection committee asking me, 'If you were faced with someone on your staff who was disruptive, what steps would you take to resolve the situation?' I said I would carefully evaluate the issue, pray about it, then try to resolve the issue. However, if that person continued to pull down the organization, I would have to let him or her go."

When I asked Brenda what she felt had been the determining factor in her being offered the job of CEO, she replied, "The selection committee saw me as a person with courage who represented a ray of hope for the community."

The next step, establishing trust, was not easy. Years of mistrust had been firmly ingrained in each stakeholder group. Brenda began with the staff she had inherited, which was in disarray. Poor morale, mistrust, and three negative and disruptive executives in key positions all posed serious obstacles for renewing the team spirit needed for progress. Brenda saw clearly the internal challenges she would be asked to address.

She proceeded to work through a very difficult process of confronting all three disruptive executives. Each one posed a unique challenge. One was extremely adversarial and threatened a lawsuit; one created dissension throughout the organization by spreading rumors; and one was a nice guy who simply was not doing his job.

"I worked closely with legal counsel to ensure I was doing the right thing according to the law," she explained.

"I addressed each executive about his specific behaviors and performance. I confronted each of the disruptive executives with tough love. I cared about them, but was brutally honest about what was expected from them to help improve the team." Brenda was honest with everyone on her staff, and she never backed down from what she felt was the right thing to do for her staff, board, and community. Ultimately, she fired the three disruptive executives whose behavior and performance were pulling down the staff.

Brenda smiled as she continued, "That was the start of a 180-degree turnaround. Team morale shot up instantly. The transformation has been incredible! Today, we have a great team." Brenda's courage and integrity in the face of adversity established trust and gave the staff new hope.

At the same time, Brenda worked to build trust with her external constituents. Her formula was simple: She took the time and effort to listen. She didn't listen through surveys or other professional tools, but one-on-one, heart-to-heart, with a caring spirit. She then started to follow through on the legitimate issues that were raised. She did not, however, do everything her constituents wanted. Instead, she made an honest assessment of her constituents' needs in terms of what was best for the common good of the community and used these as her guidelines.

"Throughout the whole process, I was met with resistance and faced some intimidating adversaries. Some tried to bully me into doing things that compromised my integrity." Brenda recalled how a local government official tried to force through a significant business development opportunity by demanding that she sign a document against her will. "He threatened to state publicly that it would be my fault if the business deal did not go through. I was intimidated, but I wasn't going to let him bully me. I held my ground and refused to sign the proposition." The official backed down, and this display of Brenda's courage and integrity helped her establish trust with many constituents within the community. People saw that Brenda was standing up to do what was right for the community, and they started to trust that her decisions weren't politically motivated.

After building this foundation of trust, Brenda felt prepared for the next stage: unifying all stakeholders toward a common goal. Her goal was to create a shared vision of hope. She told me, "We had been through so much strife; I wanted everyone to know we were a city that counted. We once had a rich tradition, and I wanted to restore that community spirit we once had."

Seeking God's wisdom enabled Brenda to not only produce significant results but to renew the spirit of a city. Since Brenda became CEO, her organization has won several awards, including the Southeast Tourism Society's "Shining Example Award," and her city has made *Facilities Magazine's* "Top 50 Convention and Visitors' Bureaus" list.

"I never gave up hope that we would get through this," said Brenda. "Once people started to see progress, they started to have hope. One thing led to another, and now our community extends its rich tradition of hospitality with pride."

Four and a half years after that difficult board planning retreat, I had the opportunity to return to Mobile to speak at their annual Tourism Day luncheon. I was so pleased to see that the community had turned 180 degrees. The ballroom proudly and elaborately displayed the city's different tourism venues. The community was working together and had tremendous hope for the future. That day, I learned to never give up hope. Brenda reminded me that, with God, we can turn what appears to be a hopeless situation into a success.

CONCLUSION

At some point in our lives, we are faced with a very difficult decision in the midst of a complicated situation. While we seek a black-and-white, ethical solution so we can do the right thing, we are forced to struggle to find a clear direction in very foggy conditions. When faced with these conditions, we may choose from one of three paths: fight, flight, or fright. We may try to solve the problem for God, run away from the problem altogether, or, like a deer frozen in headlights, do nothing, out of fear. Each of these paths is limited in scope, because the reality of our circumstances is allowed to dominate the landscape of our mind. In essence, we allow our own fears, ego, and power to cloud the potential of God's power to work though us. We feel limited by the impossible appearance of a dilemma rather than open to the new options it provides.

Linda and Brenda found themselves confronted with what appeared to be hopeless lose-lose situations. They met their challenges with courage and determination. Three characteristics helped Linda and Brenda transform a bad situation into a good solution.

1. **They sought God's wisdom first.** They never tried to solve their problems alone. Linda and Brenda sought God's wisdom before they took action and then had the personal accountability to follow through on the decisions before them.

2. **Both Linda and Brenda understood their roles, particularly their roles and responsibilities as leaders.** While knowing they were being led by a higher authority, they refused to just step back and allow fate to take over. They understood they were part of a bigger plan and that they played a role in God's important plan.

3. **They never gave up hope.** Both leaders had hope for a better future in spite of a present situation that appeared hopeless. Their personal hope created hope in others. Brenda's hope for the future of her city impacted her employees and community constituents. In time, everyone started to see progress. Eventually, she was able to transform others' thoughts away from the negative past toward a positive future.

No matter how difficult, there are times when there is no way around most of our dilemmas; we can only go through them to make the best decision. Linda and Brenda both found that it was only in the process of boldly walking through their dilemmas that solutions were found.

The process of walking through our dilemmas not only provides an eventual solution, it also defines our character. When we continue to seek God's wisdom, every step we take grows our character and brings us closer to the positive solution He has created.

DISCUSSION GUIDE

1. What is the most difficult situation or dilemma you face today?
2. When you pray for wisdom regarding this situation, what does your heart tell you?
3. Describe the underlying concerns of your dilemma.
4. Describe the ideal solution to your situation.
5. Do your thoughts, decisions, and actions align with God's principles?
6. Are you comfortable living with the consequences of your decisions?
7. Describe the direction you feel is right and start walking in that direction.

8

Servant Leadership

From getting the most out of employees to bringing out the best in employees

Whoever wants to become great among you must be your servant, and whoever wants to be first must be slave to all. For even the Son of Man did not come to be served, but to serve.

–Mark 10:43–45

Issue: How do I attract, retain, and motivate good employees?

The meeting started as usual when the General Manager's assistant broke in with the dreaded statement: "Corporate's on line one." Immediately, the General Manager picked up the phone. The Executive Committee watched as his face became ashen. We all braced ourselves for the inevitable bad news. After hanging up, he looked up and blurted, "Cut your payroll by 25 percent! I don't care how you do it—just do it! If we don't make budget by June, we'll all be out on the streets!"

At a time when customer service was named a priority, we fired a quarter of our workforce. It was a disaster. Employee morale was at an all-time low, and, as a result, customer service and our second quarter profits suffered. The employees who remained eventually cracked under the pressure. At least the Corporate Office kept their promise: They fired the entire Executive Committee. I remember us blaming the economy, the competition, and the tough labor market for our fate. We never looked at ourselves.

As we became pressured to meet a tough bottom-line, we placed demands on our employees to achieve more with less. Meanwhile, the more we looked to our employees to embrace customer service, the tougher it became to find and retain good employees who were up to the task. But then again, why would an employee want to work in a culture where there was no loyalty, respect, or trust?

Solution: Serve employees so they can serve others.

Many leaders inadvertently use employees as a means to increase profits. This subtle and misguided intent sends signals to the employee that "we care more about the customer than we care about you," and "we care more about profits than we care about you." God defines a leader as one who serves others, not one who uses others. When we serve others, we help them succeed and, by doing so, communicate, "I care more about you than profits" to our employees and customers. The result is loyal employees and long-standing customers.

In this chapter, we will meet two leaders in two different industries: Jim Bergeson, President and CEO of Colle & McVoy, Inc., and Horst Schulze, CEO of The Ritz Carlton Hotel Company. Although they have different personal styles, they each have created an organization that has attracted and kept employees who embrace service. Their solution? Servant leadership. Jim's leadership style creates an environment that promotes creativity. Horst's leadership promotes a culture of dignity and respect. Their servant leadership has created environments to which employees are drawn and in which they thrive. And the bottom line? Increased employee retention and solid profitability.

JIM BERGESON

"Bringing Out the Best in People"

Jim Bergeson is a leader who has redefined leadership. Jim is the Chairman and CEO of Colle & McVoy, Inc., one of the country's most successful marketing communication firms. Colle & McVoy provides advertising, public relations, direct marketing, interactive media, and market research for more than twenty Fortune 500 firms across the United States.

In the business world, Colle & McVoy is a model of success. The value of its stock has increased 494 percent over the last 10 years. Its client list includes 3M, Pfizer, and Medtronic. Furthermore, the company has enjoyed a steady and loyal customer base in a very competitive field. Not only does the company boast some of the finest talent in the industry, but Colle & McVoy employees are extremely loyal—a rarity in an industry where talent is hard to find and even harder to keep.

One reason for Colle & McVoy's success is that the commonly found culture of fear doesn't exist there. Jim explains, "I made sure people would not have to fear making a mistake. They would be able not only to have responsibility but also to have the authority to make a judgment call, make a decision, and even make a mistake and not fear that they will lose their job."

In his 25 years in advertising, Jim has worked with several Fortune 500 companies where fear stifled creativity, decision-making, and productivity. He saw that people were so afraid of losing their jobs that they wouldn't make decisions. He also saw courageous people who took a risk and who got fired as a result.

"I remember one client who had the courage to confront her boss regarding an ethical matter, only to be fired on the spot," Jim recalls. The VP of Marketing had approached Jim's client to review three advertising agencies for a particular job. The client clarified her assignment by asking her boss if all 14 members of her staff got to have a vote in choosing the best advertising agency. Her boss reaffirmed that everyone had a vote in choosing the right agency. The staff then spent a considerable amount of time doing research, listening to presentations, and doing painstaking evaluations to determine which agency to choose. Eleven staff members voted for one particular agency, but the boss overruled the vote and went with another agency. Jim continues, "It turned out that he had a personal friend working for one of the competing agencies, and he had my client go through the motions for appearance's sake. My client walked into the VP's office and said, 'You pulled the rug out from under me. Why didn't you just tell me the truth?' Well, she was fired. Eventually, everyone in the marketing department left."

Stories like that taught Jim what drives people away and what attracts people. "People respond to caring," he says. "It's about respecting people, believing in their capability, and giving them the freedom to contribute. I do this by leading by example. I try to model doing the right thing day-by-day, moment-to-moment. I try to seek ways to serve others."

While the title on his business card reads "Chairman and CEO," Jim describes his role as one of servant. Jim brings his faith in God to work every day through his genuine passion to serve. As a result, every single decision, action, and communication from Jim influences the culture of his organization. He has simply, yet powerfully served his employees by creating an environment in which they can thrive. Put simply, Jim didn't make Colle & McVoy successful; he helped a culture and its people be successful.

Often, leaders think servant leadership doesn't have a place in achieving bottom-line success. This couldn't be further from the truth. Serving others is good business. Jim is both a godly leader and a savvy business executive. When asked which takes precedence, people or profits, he responds, "Finding good people and treating them well makes money. In our business, our clients buy ideas and solutions. When we bring out the best in our people, they are more inspired, more creative, and can serve the customer better. That results in satisfied customers and customer loyalty, and that produces revenue."

Jim has had a dramatic influence in three areas. Since becoming CEO, Jim has created a people over profits team culture, has fostered the Colle & McVoy environment, and has helped establish the company as an employee-owned organization.

People Over Profits Team Culture—Rewarding Good People

At Colle & McVoy, an employee team is specifically created to work in partnership with each client. Each employee brings specific talents and expertise to the team and has the same goal as his or her teammates—to exceed the customer's expectations. Collectively, the team analyzes the client's needs, challenges, and goals to develop a specific strategy for solving the client's problem and achieving the client's goals. The team draws on the resources within Colle & McVoy to then customize a cost-effective solution to the problem based on the client's need.

This approach makes Colle & McVoy unique in its industry, because the customer's solution takes precedence over departmental profits. As Jim explains, "I don't believe in profit centers where each department has a selling goal. It's not in the best interest of the client. We take a long-term view of client relationships. We are not going to reward ourselves at the customer's expense. Instead, we work as one unified resource to help our customer succeed. We don't sell the customer something just to sell them something. Our business is to grow our customer's business."

This approach has added up to success for Colle & McVoy, its employees, and its clients. The employees are able to do the right thing for the customer without worrying about meeting a billing quota. In turn, this allows them to focus on the customer instead of worrying about themselves. The customer also gains, because it can trust that its best interests are at heart, rather than the vendor's profit goals.

This trust level has significantly influenced Colle & McVoy's relationships with its clients. In 1997, a client retained Colle & McVoy to launch a new arthritis pain management product for pets. With a $2,000,000 marketing budget, the client was expecting to reap $18,000,000 in sales through advertisements to veterinarians. However, after considerable analysis of the client's needs and extensive market research, the Colle & McVoy client team recommended that the company spend over $10 million to advertise directly to pet owners. Because the Colle & McVoy team had established its credibility as a trusted partner rather than a profit-driven vendor, the client agreed, risking more than five times its original budget. The campaign turned out to be a huge financial success, with well over $50,000,000 in product sales the first year, and Colle & McVoy had a very pleased customer. Everyone won.

The Colle & McVoy Environment—Growing Good People

From leadership support to the physical surroundings, the Colle & McVoy environment inspires growth. At Colle & McVoy, employees are encouraged to take risks and to be creative in helping their customers succeed. They are empowered to make decisions. They are given the freedom to communicate openly and honestly. And they are supported even if they make a mistake. This environment motivates Colle & McVoy employees.

Recently, a Colle & McVoy production manager was faced with an urgent client deadline: A new product brochure was needed ASAP. The production manager not only oversaw the weekend printing of the brochures, but he personally rented a Ryder truck and loaded it with boxes of the freshly printed brochures. After driving all night from Minneapolis to Omaha, he unloaded the truck and made sure the brochures were in the client's hands first thing Monday morning. This employee had the freedom to take risks, make decisions, and do whatever it took to help the customer succeed.

Jim knows that a basic desire of his employees is to contribute to the organization. It's his job to create an environment for this desire to grow and flourish. Therefore, Colle & McVoy employees are fully equipped with the support, resources, and authority needed to serve their customers. For example, Jim recognized that a particular team was struggling with its laptop computers. He sat down with the team and asked, "What do you need to get the job done?" They told him that, in fact, they needed three new laptops. The next morning, the team had three new laptops. Jim explains, "The added expense was peanuts in comparison to the volume of work that team produces for the client and our organization."

Colle & McVoy employees are supported even when they make a mistake. Jim described a recent incident in which a Colle & McVoy employee made a $374,000 error. Expecting to be fired, he walked into Jim's office, sat down, and said, "It was my mistake. I am sorry for it. I enjoyed working here." The employee, fully expecting that this was his last day, stood up to pack his belongings and leave when Jim stopped him. Jim told him, "Hold on. Tell me more about how the mistake was made." After hearing the story, Jim calmly told him to go back to work.

Jim took time to hear the whole story before making a judgment. By doing so, Jim reinforced four principles: (1) it's okay to make a mistake as long as it is made with good intentions; (2) honesty is required; (3) an employee should be accountable for his mistake; and (4) all persons should be treated with respect.

What kind of impact did this have on the employee? Since then, this employee has been one of the most loyal and motivated people in the company. And Jim's responsiveness has positively impacted the entire organization, clearly communicating and demonstrating honesty, respect, and accountability throughout the ranks of the organization.

In addition to creating a nurturing, supportive environment, Jim believes the physical environment greatly impacts the success of his employees. My 7:00 A.M. appointment with Jim was at Colle & McVoy's Twin Cities headquarters. I arrived early, and when the marble-walled elevator doors opened, I was greeted by a dark lobby. My gaze was immediately drawn to the orange and blue glow coming from the magnificent panoramic view of a spectacular autumn sunrise through a massive wall of glass. Twenty-four floors below, the radiant fall colors were intensified by the sun's glow as the morning came to life. I found myself excited and inspired. The early morning sunlight filtered into the office, displaying a warm and beautiful environment filled with rich woodwork, etched glass, and open space. What a wonderful way to start a workday! A few minutes later Jim walked in. I couldn't help but mention that the office space must have cost a fortune. He nodded in agreement and said, "Creating a satisfying work environment helps people thrive. It's my job to create an environment that fosters creativity and growth."

The design of a work environment reflects a company's attitude toward its employees. Colle & McVoy's physical space reflects a total commitment to employee growth, creativity, and service to others. Every inch of space seems to serve that commitment. The beautiful reception area makes customers and guests feel welcome.

The door to each employee's office features the employee's photograph in lieu of the typical name plate. Angled offices instead of square cubicles, natural sunlight, comfortable seating, and many other little accoutrements foster creativity.

In an era in which companies demand more and more from their employees, it's puzzling that they don't invest in workspaces that will boost productivity and, ultimately, loyalty. Wise leaders who care for employees know that external conditions impact internal motivation and productivity. Jim knows that spending money on a work environment is simply a wise investment.

The Colle & McVoy ESOP—Keeping Good People

From coast to coast, companies espouse the virtues of employee ownership. The words ring a noble tune, but few companies back it up with dollars. Colle & McVoy, an established ESOP (Employee Stock Ownership Plan) company, is owned by its employees. Employees share in the growth of Colle & McVoy through ownership of its common stock. After a year of service, employees first become owners, and after five years are 100 percent vested in their shares. (This is highly unusual in the advertising industry, where most firms are owned by one or two people.)

Has this concept worked? The bottom line speaks for itself. Since the ESOP was established in 1989, Colle &

McVoy's stock has more than doubled twice. Colle & McVoy was named national ESOP Company of the Year in 1997.

In the communications industry, where talented employees hop from company to company like free agents in professional sports, employee retention and loyalty is a key issue. The Colle & McVoy ESOP has been an anchor for keeping talented people for three primary reasons. First, it's profitable; Colle & McVoy has shattered its pre-ESOP growth goals. Second, employees literally own the company. Each employee knows that his or her efforts will influence both the success and the future direction of the company. Finally, the ESOP causes Colle & McVoy employees to work together to solve common business and personal issues.

Beyond the tangible incentives that contribute to employee loyalty, the Colle & McVoy ESOP creates the stability that employees look for. Kim Fox, Vice President of Accounts, contrasts being an employee-owner versus an employee to owning versus renting a home: "You take better care of the things you own." [1]

At Colle & McVoy, employee meetings and receptions are used to recognize valuable contributions to the company. Informal gatherings are designed to reinforce the behaviors that define the organization's culture. Jim specifically looks for behaviors that reflect Colle & McVoy values and then goes out of his way to reward and recognize those values. For example, EE Awards, which include recognition at a company gathering and a tangible reward, are given to employees who exceed client expectations.

Through the creation of a people-over-profits team culture, a supportive environment, and an employee-owned company, Jim has servant-led Colle & McVoy to both financial success and a high retention rate of some of the most talented employees in the marketing/advertising industry. His servant leadership approach brings out the best in Colle & McVoy's employees. (Postscript: Colle & McVoy remained an ESOP Company until March 1999, when a majority interest in the company was sold.)

HORST SCHULZE
"An Uncompromising Respect for People"

It's very clear where Horst Schulze's passion lies. He has an uncompromising respect for people, borne out of his love for God. Horst honors a basic biblical principle: By enhancing employees' self-worth and dignity, he enhances their ability to provide exceptional service to their customers. This core value, providing respect and dignity for every human being, has helped The Ritz Carlton Hotel Company, of which he is CEO, become one of the most successful hotel chains in the world.

"We are ladies and gentlemen serving ladies and gentlemen"; the Ritz Carlton motto defines how the company values each employee, as well as the service those employees provide to their customers. This principle works. Whereas the standard hospitality industry employee turnover rate is in excess of 100 percent per year, the Ritz Carlton Hotel Company boasts a turnover rate of only 29 percent. In 1992, it became the first hospitality organization to receive the Malcolm Baldridge National Quality Award. Ritz Carlton remains an outstanding success story and an industry leader in employee satisfaction, customer satisfaction, and profitability.

But Horst's servant leadership is not soft. A leader who cares about people doesn't have to care less about the bottom line. Horst is a demanding leader who sets extremely high standards of excellence, quality, and service and who expects that Ritz Carlton will be regarded as the quality and market leader in the hotel industry. Horst explains, "When making decisions, I ask myself: Is it good for all concerned—God, the organization, the employees, the customers, and vendors? If yes, then drive it forward relentlessly."

Horst expects an equally demanding commitment to the respect and dignity for every employee in the Ritz Carlton organization. "I demand from every manager that every employee be respected fully as a human being," he says. "I make it very clear that no one can claim to be a better human being than another. A dishwasher is as important in this organization as a vice president."

The key to Horst's success lies in how he weaves biblical principles and values, including respect, caring, trust, fairness, and teamwork, into the fabric of his organization. These values and principles have become the foundation for Ritz Carlton's success, as measured by employee retention, customer satisfaction, and profitability.

The concluding paragraph of the Ritz Carlton mission statement reads:

We will always select employees who share our values. We will strive to meet individual needs because our success depends on the satisfaction, effort, and commitment of each employee. Our leaders will constantly support and energize all employees to continuously improve productivity and customer satisfaction. This will be accomplished by creating an environment of genuine care, trust, respect, fairness, and teamwork through training, education, empowerment, participation, recognition, rewards, and career opportunities.

Horst and Ritz Carlton leadership have created a system that enables every employee to connect with the organization's core values in a powerful and meaningful way. Four primary components, including the employee selection process, involved leadership, training and education, and daily communication, have turned these values and goals into a living reality.

The Employee Selection Process

Horst explains that Ritz Carlton takes the time to select the right people for the right job and doesn't hire someone just to fill a position. "Our industry is notorious for getting bodies to fulfill a function—do things," he says. "I think it is irresponsible and in a sense immoral. People should not just fulfill a function. They have a right to be a part of something."

Ritz Carlton uses a highly sophisticated selection process to determine the character traits needed to fulfill a particular position, as well as to determine the ability of a candidate to meet the specific job requirements. In essence, the company takes a painstaking amount of effort to see if there is both a competency and values fit. Horst explains, "There needs to be the right fit for the employee and the organization. The same is true with our values. It is important that the employee believes in the same values as we do."

This up-front effort has produced enormous back-end results. Incorporation of this selection process alone contributed to a 50 percent drop in Ritz Carlton's turnover rate.

Involved Leadership

Horst Schulze demands a lot from himself and his fellow leaders. He tells people, "Leadership sets the vision, the standards, the values, and goals of the organization, and then we caringly involve every single employee in the process. We do that by living the values—sharing them slowly, carefully, and properly."

Leadership's role, Horst insists, is to "support and energize" employees to continuously improve productivity and customer satisfaction. This is done by demonstrating the values and modeling the correct way. At Ritz Carlton, it is every manager's responsibility to work side by side with his or her employees.

When opening a new hotel, Horst personally communicates the organization's values. "Every hotel we have opened, I have opened," he says. "I have helped train the maids, the waiters, and so on. I will stay for 10 days so they know that I am there to be with them. And I will tell them, 'Yes, I'm important,' and then I will point to each and every employee and say, 'but so are you, and you, and you.'"

Training and Education

Ritz Carlton provides over 100 hours of training and education to each employee. The focus of this training is on the company's core values. "It is critical that the values are clearly understood by everyone," explains Horst. The organization has developed "Our Gold Standards," which clearly define the vision, values, goals, and methodology of Ritz Carlton. These Gold Standards include:

The Credo: reinforces the priority and commitment toward service

The Three Steps to Service: further define the specific activities and decisions of customer interface

The Ritz Carlton Basics: 20 points that focus entirely on guest problem-solving and help eliminate internal competition

The Ritz Carlton Motto: reinforces the values of respect, dignity, and service

Daily Communication

"We have created a system that reinforces our values to every one of our 16,000 employees every single day," explains Horst. Ritz Carlton has a daily program called the line-up. Every day, for every shift, an employee meeting is held that provides an opportunity for employees to communicate, from getting instructions for the day to solving problems. In addition to the necessary communication that takes place at the hotel level, the corporate office sends out a daily message that reinforces their goals and values. These messages help the employee grow, personally and professionally. "For example," says Horst, "a message will pass on congratulations to specific employees on anniversary dates, or they will provide tips on dealing with stress, or provide an inspirational quote of the day."

Horst Schulze turned his uncompromising respect for people into a successful culture. His servant leadership, with its focus on biblical principles and values, has helped make The Ritz Carlton Hotel Company a worldwide leader.

CONCLUSION

While the business world commonly attempts to address employee attraction and retention issues by implementing programs with a hit or miss approach, that's not the solution. The solution to the issue of attracting and retaining employees who embrace the model of service is a paradigm shift in our definition of leadership.

The customer service level and organizational commitment of your employees is directly influenced by your definition of leadership. The business world commonly defines leadership as being one of the most powerful and influential persons in the organization. In other words, a leader is first among many. Being amongst the most powerful in an organization, a leader's job includes directing others.

The biblical definition of leadership says "whoever wants to become great among you must be your servant, and whoever wants to be first must be slave of all. For even the Son of Man did not come to be served, but to serve" (Mark 10:43–45). God clearly states that a leader puts the needs of all others before his own needs. Instead of directing others, God defines a leader as one who serves others.

Servant leadership became a business term during the 1970s, when Robert Greenleaf coined the phrase "servant-leader." He defined the servant-leader as one who is a servant first, a leader who desires to make sure other people's needs are being served. At first glance, being a servant-leader is contradictory to success in a highly competitive, bottom-line world, but servant leadership is the tool God gave leaders to succeed. Everything God designs is a perfect and trustworthy blueprint for success.

ACNielsen, a market research and analysis firm, has conducted regular employee surveys and linked the results with customer satisfaction data. ACNielsen has found that when employee satisfaction rises, financial results improve. A financial services unit at Monsanto conducted baseline customer and employee satisfaction surveys. They found that employee satisfaction with work/life balance and general job satisfaction were the two strongest predictors of customer satisfaction.[2]

Jim Bergeson and Horst Schulze are very different leaders. They come from different backgrounds, work in diverse industries, and have different personal styles and approaches to servant leadership. Jim created an environment that inspired the creativity within his employees, and Horst raised the standard of service of Ritz Carlton employees. Regardless of approach, style, and industry, they were each business successes because they found a way to bring out the best in their employees. As a result, each of their organizations has enjoyed the benefits of low employee turnover, increased customer satisfaction, and long-term growth and profitability.

Despite their differences, these men and their organizations share some commonalities:

- While their source of inspiration is found in their faith in God, they were able to communicate the core principles to their workforce in a meaningful and nonthreatening way.
- Each leader demonstrated the values of respect, integrity, and service through leadership by example.

- The importance of these core principles was demonstrated through the commitment of time, energy, training, and money.
- Jim and Horst each said that helping the employee succeed was the key to customer service and business success. They each consistently backed this philosophy with action.
- Each created an atmosphere that equipped and enabled the employee to succeed, whether it was in the selection process, training, or the environment.
- Their internal systems were based on a long-term process, not a short-term program.
- For Colle & McVoy and The Ritz Carlton Hotel Company, servant leadership has worked. Employees are attracted and retained, customers are satisfied, and the companies are profitable.

This personal action plan is designed to help leaders by providing practical suggestions for attracting and retaining employees:

Personal Action Plan

Step One: Create a business philosophy statement that aligns the organization's beliefs with its actions.

It is very important to align what we believe with what we do. This alignment between our beliefs and actions will be the foundation on which we build employee loyalty. Our goal is twofold: to create a statement that communicates our philosophy to our employees and to establish our credibility by defining the actions we will take that support our philosophy.

Before we create a philosophy statement, we need to identify our credibility gap. If we have an existing mission statement, we need to ask ourselves, "Do our behaviors and actions align with the present mission of the organization?" "Do our outcomes match our promises?" This requires an honest assessment of the gaps between what is presently written and how we run our business. The assessment process can range from an informal review to a formal 360-degree feedback analysis.

Once we've identified the credibility gap, we're ready to create a philosophy statement. In the statement, identify the beliefs, values, and principles that drive our business decisions and document how we will lead others to achieve our organization's goals.

Step Two: Create an environment for growth.

Once we have created the foundation in which to communicate our beliefs, we need to create a framework with which to connect our employees in a meaningful way.

If we believe that maximizing people's potential translates to maximizing profit potential, then we need to design a system or process that enables employees not only to do their jobs more effectively but also to contribute beyond their personal expectations. As seen in the two case studies, the profiled organizations not only designed room for employee growth, they created an expectation for growth. In essence, they designed a system that grows people.

Starting with a flip chart, we need to create a flow chart to demonstrate how our organization makes money. Remember to include every step, from sales to production to delivery to our customer. Identify all the employees in the process, and check every system, procedure, and communication.

Then we should ask ourselves; does the system help or hinder employee growth and service to the customer? If we identify a hindrance, locate where the obstacle is found. From each step, make two lists; one titled "What's Working" and the other titled "What's Not Working." Within each list, identify the parts of the process that help and hinder employee growth and customer service.

Once every department in our organization has gone through the same process, we need to hold a brainstorming session. Using the flip chart heading "Personal Growth That Contributes to Organizational Growth," ask each employee and department to complete the same information:

My untapped talents are . . .
If I had the freedom to fail, I would (fill in blank) to help make this organization better.
I can best contribute by . . .

Compile the information gathered from all employees. We need to ask our leaders and employees to develop a plan that will grow both the employee and the organization.

Step Three: Develop the four R's that bring out the best in employees: resources, respect, recognition, and rewards.

Now that we've created a foundation of beliefs and a framework for connecting others to these shared values, we now need to reinforce the employee behaviors that honor the organization's philosophy. Specifically, we need to reinforce the behavior rather than the result. A common mistake leaders make is to reward the result instead of the behavior that achieved the result. Naturally, that reinforces the wrong message, one that says, "I don't care how you get to the bottom-line (even if you step on toes or are deceitful), just as long as you get there." When we focus on the principle over the result, we reinforce the importance and meaning of the principle itself. When we recognize and reward the principles and values that elevate people, we liberate employees to raise their standards of excellence to a higher level. This process builds a culture of employees who have the freedom to be creative, take risks, and strive toward continuous improvement.

We can simplify our roles as servant leaders by creating a daily focus on the four R's.

1. **Resources:** Identify the resources needed to maximize our employees' performance. Resources can

include training, technical support, and financial support, among others. Identification of needed resources starts by asking our employees what they need to do their jobs better.

2. **Respect:** Respect begins with recognizing the employee as a unique individual rather than a body filling a job. As we have seen from the case studies, finding both the right skills fit and the right values fit is a very important piece to employee retention. Consistent communication between leadership and employees is essential for a continued partnership between organization and employee.

3. **Recognition:** Recognition for a job well done is one of the greatest reinforcers of good behavior. Even better, recognition can be free. Most employees are looking for recognition for their contributions. Create a daily plan to recognize contributions. This will motivate the employee and help shape the desired behavior we are looking for.

4. **Reward:** The best way to reward employees is to ask our employees how they like to be rewarded. Remember, everyone is different. Some people like to be recognized publicly, some privately. Have each employee identify small tangible rewards (food, gift certificates, plaques) and intangible rewards (pat on the back, verbal praise) and create

ways to celebrate individual and team victories along the way.

Servant leadership is the key to attracting, retaining, and motivating good employees. Leaders who create an environment that appreciates employees' talents, helps them grow, and brings out their best, will, like Jim Bergeson and Horst Schulze, reap the reward of loyal, long-term employees. Serving the servant will help your employees and your organization succeed.

DISCUSSION GUIDE

1. How do you define the quality and integrity of "service" in your organization?
2. How do you define servant leadership?
3. How would you define your leadership role?
4. What is your toughest challenge when it comes to finding and keeping employees?
5. Identify the most important lesson you learned from the two case studies.
6. Identify one action you will take to improve employee satisfaction.
7. Identify one action you will take to improve the level of service in your organization.

Notes

1. Karen Lund, "Owners at Every Corner," *Minnesota Business & Opportunities* (August 1997).
2. Sue Shellenberger, "Surveys Link Satisfaction of Employees, Customers," *Wall Street Journal* as published by *Star Tribune* (January 25, 1999).

9

Integration

From balancing people and profits to integrating people and profits

Teach them the decrees and laws, and show them the way to live and the duties they are to perform.

–Exodus 18:20

Issue: How do I balance employee needs with profit obligations?

s Senior Vice President, Ron had performed admirably through a difficult year of restructuring and downsizing. When we met, I found a tired leader. Ron said, "Larry, I'm tired of deciding other people's fates. It's taken its toll on me. I've decided to resign." Ron had worked compassionately with hundreds of good employees as they lost their jobs, but one particular incident had caused him to make the drastic decision to step away from his job.

Fran was one of the division leaders struggling to keep her job. She was a good leader, but she was young and had been placed in a difficult situation where she had to develop credibility fast. Unfortunately, her husband died suddenly of a heart attack. She tried desperately both to deal with her grief and to work through her leadership issues. He did whatever he could for Fran and gave her as much time and latitude as possible.

Unfortunately, Fran was not responding to the business demands, and the pressure from the company president was growing. As difficult as it was to admit, Ron knew that Fran's situation was hurting the division's performance. Ron made the painful business decision to fire Fran. For Ron, it was the straw that broke the camel's back. He was tired of dealing with dilemmas which caused him to choose between people and profits. Ron resigned shortly thereafter.

Solution: Integrate people and profits into win-win solutions.

As leaders, we struggle with dilemmas such as Ron's, dilemmas in which there are no easy answers. It would be easy to blame the bottom-line pressure of deadlines and profit obligations as the culprits for employee and leadership burnout. But we know that there will always be tension between people's needs and profit obligations. The key to our success in this area is not in trying to balance these two sometimes opposing dynamics (people and profits), but to integrate these two dynamics so we can create win-win solutions.

In this chapter we will look at two leaders, Andrea Ritchie and Ken Melrose, who have learned how to integrate employee needs and profit obligations. Andrea Ritchie, President of Northwestern Travel Management, a corporate travel management service, struggled to balance the people/profit dilemma. We'll take a snapshot of how she made her decision and how her actions solved her problem. Ken Melrose, CEO of The Toro Company, a leading manufacturer of turf maintenance equipment including mowers, aerators, and irrigation systems, guides us on his 25-year journey to learn how to integrate people's needs and profit obligations in a large organization. These case studies will give us both a snapshot and wide-angle view of this challenging dilemma.

ANDREA RITCHIE

"Changing Win-Lose Dilemmas into Win-Win Solutions"

A ndrea Ritchie, President of Northwestern Travel Management, faced one of the most difficult dilemmas of her life. The company had lost one of its biggest accounts and was faced with the need to downsize by laying off 30 employees. Downsizing made good business sense in the short term in order to remain competitive, and Andrea felt the pressure to move quickly. Recalling the situation, Andrea says, "I felt a tremendous burden to make the right decision. Not only did I have 30 families at stake, but I was toying with the other employees' compensation." Rather than make a quick business decision, she sought God's wisdom and perspective on the situation first. In prayer, Andrea posed some questions that weighed heavily on her heart: "Lord, how much profit is enough? How do I balance my obligation to make a profit with my obligation to our employees who have been so loyal and worked so hard for this organization? Do I let my bottom line look bad, or do I lay off people?"

Andrea prayerfully weighed the big-picture reward of doing what she thought was right against the short-term risks of trying to make up the lost revenue required to keep the division afloat. "I didn't know what to do," she recalls. "I was really torn. I just couldn't see letting go of good employees. It didn't seem fair! We have a great team of loyal, hard-working employees. It's not only going to affect those who are laid off, this is going to affect everyone."

She felt a sense of urgency about making her decision. While Andrea knew she didn't have the luxury of time, she was wise enough not to struggle with this decision alone. She reached out in many directions: She prayed to God for wisdom, and she discussed the dilemma with her husband and a few close friends. Andrea consulted with key sales-people on her team to strategize options. She also went outside her organization to seek counsel.

I met Andrea through ChurchMetro, an organization whose mission is to serve business leaders by advancing biblically based solutions. I facilitated ChurchMetro's CEO discussion groups, where leaders would share and discuss their most pressing moral and ethical dilemmas. Andrea was a regular attendee, and in one particular discussion group she shared her dilemma. I saw Andrea demonstrate her true leadership qualities as she asked tough questions, such as, "How much profit is enough?" She allowed herself to be transparent so her peers could ask her tough questions in return. It was evident that she took this decision seriously, and she was actively seeking wise advice from respected peers.

After much reflection, prayer, and consultation with her colleagues, Andrea made the decision not to lay off the 30 employees and, instead, to face the pressure of trying to recoup the lost revenue. Once the decision had been made, Andrea felt a definitive peace and confidence that she had done the right thing.

But making the decision was only half the battle. Andrea next had to communicate the issue and her decision to both the owner and the chief operating officer. Although she didn't tell them about her prayers, she explained what she had determined was the right thing to do, and she provided a clear, specific, and well-thought-out plan for rebuilding sales.

Andrea reflected on how doing the right moral thing and the right financial thing came together before her big presentation. "My faith gave me the strength to make this happen," says Andrea. "After much prayer, I first decided to do the right moral thing for our employees by keeping them, then I came up with the argument to justify my decision."

Andrea asserted that the organization had invested a tremendous amount of time and energy in training these 30 employees. Over time, these employees had become valuable professionals who understood the real meaning of customer service and teamwork. Andrea reasoned that the short-term higher payroll would be a small price in comparison to the long-term dollars required to locate, hire, and train new employees to support the company's future new accounts. In addition, keeping these already-valuable employees meant better efficiency and profit margins, enabling the sales staff to go back to each of the accounts they were developing and offer better financial packages. Andrea calculated, "If this enriched financial offer lands the majority of the proposals we have outstanding, we will get the $40 million in sales needed to offset our short-term loss."

When I asked Andrea how she got both executives to agree, she provided two reasons:

1. **Her decision combined an understanding of what was right with a God-centered perspective of the bottom-line risks.** When Andrea prayed for wisdom, she asked, "Lord, is the risk worth taking to justify doing the right thing?" In short, she carefully sought God's wisdom by asking the right question. As a result, her decision wasn't just the morally correct thing to do; it was a wise, well-thought-through business decision as well.

2. **Her conviction for doing the right thing and her confidence that the organization could rise to the challenge created a faith in her that outweighed the fear of the short-term risk.** Andrea says, "Once I made the decision, I never doubted. There were no anxieties, no fears. I

truly believed that we would pick up new business to offset this loss."

Although both of the other executives were bottom-line
businessmen, they ultimately supported Andrea's decision.
The three executives then got in a car and drove to the
office together to communicate their unified decision to all
their employees.

When they arrived at the office, they were met with
nervous anticipation. The team knew something bad had
happened, but they didn't know what. The owner, John,
broke the news that they had lost the account. Andrea
recalls, "They were in shock. They were numb." Then she
remembers hearing, in almost the same sentence, John state
emphatically, "You all have a job here—every one of you.
You have nothing to worry about." The chief operating
officer, Art, spoke next and reinforced the same message.
Art reiterated how much they valued their employees' contributions. To show their support, the executives divided the
employees into three small groups, listened to their concerns, and answered all of their questions.

And the support continued after that eventful day.
Even though all of the employees heard the message that
their jobs were secure, they still had doubts and fears.
Andrea recalled that she visited the office a couple of
times each week for the next three months to answer
more questions, give further assurance, and provide
encouragement.

Andrea grinned broadly as she told me the rest of the story. All of the organization's employees pulled together to meet the challenge before them. As for the 30 employees, Andrea states, "Once they got their questions answered, they became gung-ho. I asked for 10 percent improvement in productivity, and I got 24 percent!" In a short time, the sales department came through with flying colors and produced the sales needed to offset the loss of the key account.

Andrea's decision has had positive and profitable results. Not only has the company benefited financially, but the trust and morale of the organization have been strengthened considerably. In addition to the bottom-line success, turnover is at an all-time low and loyalty is at an all-time high. And as new employees join Northwestern Travel Management, Andrea's story is shared, perpetuating a culture of employee and management trust.

Andrea solved her dilemma by bringing people together. Rather than suffering with her dilemma alone, she facilitated a series of discussions with the right stakeholders and peers to find a solution. Together, they discovered both the right moral thing to do and the right financial thing to do. Andrea's story demonstrates that leaders need not suffer alone with a tough issue. Through wisdom, we can turn what appears to be a win-lose situation into a win-win solution.

KEN MELROSE
"From Profits First to People First"

Ken Melrose, Chairman and CEO of The Toro Company, felt very alone as a leader in the 1970s. His focus was different from the typical 1970s leader. He cared deeply about employees, but the popular management theory of the time focused more on profitability. Ken recognized a significant disparity between what he believed in church on Sunday and how he and his coworkers behaved on Monday. He recalls, "I felt called to change the way I behaved in the workplace, and, as a leader, I felt compelled to influence the way others treated one another also."

"It was uncomfortable and awkward at the very least to communicate the biblical principles of servant leadership at a time when talking about God was taboo," Ken explains. "However, the Christian model is to put yourself in awkward and uncomfortable positions and just have faith that God is leading you where He wants you to go." Ken took some risks, like starting a leadership group at Toro that incorporated biblical principles on decision-making, power, and hierarchy. The group discussed different ways to make decisions that impact the bottom line, but also that value people and are honest and ethical. That was 25 years ago. Since then, Ken's visibility, which started out very quiet and subdued, has become more prominent, and, as a result, the company has done well.

When Ken became CEO of Toro, a manufacturer of home lawn care and turf management products, it was already a market leader. But he inherited a culture in which employees were used as a means to get results, and management did whatever it took to achieve the bottom line.

Remarkably, Ken transformed a traditional, bottom-line company into a successful Fortune 500 firm with a turnover rate less that half the national average. His story describes how a leader can integrate employee needs and profit obligations into win-win solutions.

A New Leadership Philosophy—From "Profits First" to "People First"

When Ken became CEO, he deliberately set out to redefine the corporate culture from a "profits first" to a "people first" mentality. Ken knew in his heart that maximizing the potential of his employees would eventually translate to bottom-line success. As he writes in his book, *Making the Grass Greener on Your Side,* "My personal philosophy is this: Everyone has the potential to contribute to achieving the goals of the company. If you can unleash that potential, market leadership and financial success will be natural by-products."[1]

Ken explains that Toro decided to build a business philosophy that focused on putting the employee first. "If you take care of your employees, and eliminate obstacles and barriers to their success," says Ken, "then you will be in a better position to satisfy the customer. And if you satisfy the customer, you will obtain market leadership. And market leadership helps contribute to being an economically healthy and profitable company."

A new philosophy statement was the first step toward changing Toro's culture. The statement served a dual purpose: It communicated a new way of achieving business success, and it provided a blueprint for all employees to be included in the process. The statement reads as follows:

> We believe the single most important factor that influences our success as a company is the Toro employee. Therefore, it is our privilege and responsibility to create a culture and an environment that supports and encourages individuals at Toro to achieve their highest potential. In order for employees to achieve that potential, we accept the responsibility to show by our actions that we care about them as individuals, understand their needs, recognize their talents, and support them in their efforts to grow and change. At the same time, all of us employees must accept responsibility for our own performance and foster the environment that facilitates this accountability.

As a company, and as the people of Toro, we pledge
to execute this philosophy genuinely and with excellence. By doing so, we believe that Toro will be most
successful in meeting its overall corporate goals.[2]

This document became the standard for the organization's
behaviors and decisions.

A New Leadership Style—Servant Leadership

After stating their new business philosophy, Ken new
that they needed to find a way to execute it. "We needed to
find a realistic way to back up our rhetoric," says Ken. So
after agreeing on this new philosophy, Ken and his executive team asked themselves, "What kind of leadership style
allows the employee to be his or her potential best?"

They began by looking for a leadership philosophy that
enhanced the productivity of Toro's employees. "Servant
leadership came about partly from my Christian beliefs and
partly because our executive team knew our employees
could do their jobs better than we could do them, and it
made sense to empower and involve them in the process of
growing our business," explains Ken.

A Leadership Challenge—Helping Leaders Change

Next came the toughest challenge: teaching leaders and
managers to serve employees. It was clear that leadership

and middle management had the primary role of unleashing the potential of employees, but how does a leader significantly influence the behavior of managers who have been rewarded for directing and controlling employees for years? How should they be retrained? How were they to be evaluated? On the bottom line or on employee growth?

Ken found the answer by studying the leadership attributes of Jesus. "If you were to study Christ as a business leader, you would discover the leadership skills needed in business today," says Ken, "being visionary, being a good communicator, having good listening skills, and motivating people."

Ken found that the best way to train his leaders and managers was by example. His inspiration to demonstrate servant-leadership came from learning how Jesus washed the feet of his disciples. "As the leader," Ken explains, "I focus on visible ways of walking the talk as a means to influence leaders and managers. As an example, our officers and directors will periodically walk around the corporate offices serving coffee and donuts, or we will visit our plants and work side-by-side with the workers assembling and building components. In fact, we try to show our vulnerability by demonstrating that we can't do the job as well as the person who owns the job." Ken recognized that demonstrating servant-leadership was not enough, however. He had to create ways to back up his examples with more widespread action. He didn't want lip service; he wanted people to utilize servant-leadership to solve difficult dilemmas.

One major challenge for leaders and managers was their obligation to both serve employees and make a profit. They saw this as an either/or dilemma and tried to find a balance between profit and people. Instead, Ken challenged his managers to integrate results and relationships into win-win solutions. "The more you tenaciously persevere in integrating these two sides, the better you get as a leader," he affirms.

One example of a people-versus-profits dilemma occurred at a plant in Shakopee, Minnesota, that was faced with seasonal business swings. Toro management struggled with the idea of laying off the plant's employees. Coincidentally, the company was having a problem with a product in the field at the same time. Leaders decided to temporarily move the plant's employees into the field to help distributors solve the problem. These employees went out into the parks and golf courses and worked directly with Toro's customers. This alternative was a win-win solution for everyone: Toro's customers were happy, the employees not only continued to work but also received a great learning experience, and the decision was a profitable one.

To reinforce the new servant-leadership approach, a new performance appraisal system was developed, and financial rewards were modified to align with the new corporate philosophy and values. Helping others succeed became an important measure of success. A large portion of senior managers' incentive compensation was changed to reflect how well they practiced the Toro philosophy, as judged by their peers and subordinates.

As behavior began to change, the benefits of servant-leadership started to filter through The Toro Company, from leaders to middle managers to employees. Ken explains, "I try to demonstrate leadership in a way that models the expected behaviors so that other leaders are encouraged to do the same thing with their staff, and this cascades throughout the organizational structure. What you end up with is managers not trying to direct and control their people, but trying to coach and serve their people to be more motivated and empowered, and to get better and better in what they do."

When Ken is asked to identify the one thing that has made the most difference over the past 20 years, he names trust. He believes that creating an environment where people trust each other is one of the most important aspects of servant-leadership and one that gives terrific bottom-line results. "People in a trusting environment will stand up and say, 'You can count on me.' It creates a bias for action. It allows the employee to take risks and actions to do what is right," Ken says.

The Payoff—Employee Retention

Ken's leadership philosophy has resulted in a dramatic cultural change and unprecedented growth. After 20 years of perseverance and commitment to servant leadership, in

1998 Toro enjoyed a turnover ratio that was less than half the national average.

"Why do our employees want to work for us?" Ken offers. "Most people want to value other people and produce quality work. They want to work in an environment that values trust and respect. They want to work for someone who is trustworthy, where they can take a risk and not get hammered, and be accountable without having to fear getting burned. There is great potential in all our employees to do quality work if we allow them to."

Ken's leadership is based on three key attributes: faith, courage, and perseverance. His faith created a calling and conviction to live godly principles at a time when it was taboo. His courage enabled him to take risks by teaching servant-leadership at a time when it went completely against contemporary leadership theory. His perseverance helped him to build a successful Fortune 500 company with over 4,800 employees where people are respected and appreciated, and profits remain solid. After 25 years of commitment to helping employees grow, Ken and Toro are realizing the fruits of their labor.

CONCLUSION

Integration is the bringing together of separate parts into a whole. As leaders, our role is to bring together people to achieve the company's mission and to make a profit. Our job is not to judge between people and profits; our job is to facilitate the process of these two elements coming together.

Organizations have made sweeping changes, such as rightsizing and downsizing, without ever including the employees affected in the process. In essence, leaders have been taught a win-lose system in which the leader is forced to be judge and jury, balancing people's needs on one side and profit obligations on the other. Ken Melrose attributes one strategy as the key to his success: He challenged, taught, and showed his employees and leaders how to integrate relationships and results into win-win solutions.

Exodus 18:20 is but one verse in a biblical story that illustrates the common challenge faced by leaders. Moses, leader of the Israelites, was a conscientious leader who tried to do it all. Leading about 2 million people, he was the one and only person making final decisions regarding how to run this new nation of people. Moses was getting burned out trying to make all the decisions. One day, Moses' father-in-law, Jethro, came to him with some wise advice.

> When his father-in-law saw all that Moses was doing for the people, he said, "What is this you are doing for the people? Why do you sit as judge, while all these people stand around you from morning till evening?

Moses answered him, "Because the people come to see me to seek God's will. Whenever they have a dispute, it is brought to me, and I decide between the parties and inform them of God's decrees and laws.

Moses' father-in-law replied, "What you are doing is not good. You and these people who come to you will only wear yourselves out. The work is too heavy for you; you cannot handle it alone. Listen now to me, and I will give you some advice, and may God be with you. You must be the people's representative before God and bring their disputes to him. Teach them the decrees and laws, and show them the way to live and the duties they are to perform. But select capable men from all people—men who fear God, trustworthy men who hate dishonest gain—and appoint them as officials over thousands, hundreds, fifties, and tens. Have them serve as judges for the people at all times, but have them bring every difficult case to you; the simple cases they can decide for themselves. That will make your load lighter, because they will share it with you. If you do this and God so commands, you will be able to stand the strain, and all these people will go home satisfied. (Exodus 18:14–23)

These verses provide insights and principles as they relate to our roles within our organizations.

- We are the people's representative before God (we can pray for our employees).
- We cannot handle it alone (we will not succeed trying to solve the people/profit issue alone).
- We must make sure our mission defines the values and principles that drive the organization.
- We show others the way (we train our employees to integrate people and profits).
- We delegate the decision-making to trustworthy leaders of character.
- We create an expectation of shared responsibility and accountability to achieve the common mission.
- As we follow this plan within God's will, the result will be an outcome that will benefit both us and our employees.

It's important to understand that integrating people's needs and company profit obligations is an ongoing process of bringing people together to achieve a greater good. In Andrea's case, we see her prayerfully weighing the moral and financial options alone, yet ultimately including every single employee as part of the solution. In Ken's story, he integrated every employee, from senior leader to line employee, into the process of serving the mission and achieving profits. The first and last sentence of the Toro philosophy statement clearly state the intention of the organization and what is expected of each employee: "We believe the single most important factor that influences success is the Toro employee. At the same time, all of us employees must accept responsibility for our own performance and foster the environment that facilitates this accountability."

Andrea and Ken show us how important the leader is in facilitating the process of integrating people and profits. Helping others integrate these two dynamic factors goes beyond delegating authority and empowering others; it's in challenging others to work together for a greater good. The following tool, the Four Ps of a High-Performing Partnership, will help you integrate people and profits into win-win solutions.

The Four Ps of a High-Performing Partnership

1. Purpose

What is the common mission and shared vision we both are working toward?

The organizational mission statement should be a common mission that every employee relates to and finds meaningful. The better an employee understands how he or she contributes to the mission, the more invested he or she will become in its success. It's also important for the leader and the employee to have a shared vision of success. In other words, each party must see a benefit in the relationship. This is where it is important to tie the performance of the employee to the financial performance of the organization. Making this connection helps to define the employee's goals.

2. Positions

What do we specifically expect of each other as we work toward our shared vision and mission?

It's important to consistently clarify roles, responsibilities, and expectations between employee and leader. This becomes particularly critical in times of change. The more you clarify expectations with an associate up front, the less you will be confronted with difficult decisions and misunderstandings.

3. Process

How will we work together to achieve the results we identified?

Process describes how each party—employee and leader—will work together to create results. A good process provides an effective road map for people to work together.

4. Performance

How will we measure our success?

Both leader and employee need to define success in terms of relationships (employee and customer relationships) and results (financial goals). Both are important and need to be discussed in terms of how they align with the organizational mission.

In summary, the people/profits dilemma will always involve a level of creative tension that will challenge us. As caring, compassionate leaders, we will always have certain cases that pull at our heartstrings. But as Jethro told Moses, we are not in this situation alone. With God's guidance, with our facilitation skills, and with capable people around us, we will create the best possible win-win solutions that serve the greater good.

DISCUSSION GUIDE

1. How do you create a common mission and a shared vision of success between you and your employees?
2. Is the mission statement and shared vision meaningful to all parties? Do employees see how their contribution provides both a personal and organizational benefit?
3. Is the fate of your employees in your hands alone, or is there a shared accountability for success?
4. How do you communicate your expectations for both results and relationships to your employees?

5. How do you measure employee contributions for achieving tasks and working with others?
6. How do you reward employee performance for both results and successful relationships?

Notes

1. Kendrick B. Melrose, *Making the Grass Greener on Your Side* (San Francisco: Berrett-Koehler, 1995), 37.
2. Ibid, 145.

10

Priorities

From burning out
to rekindling your spirit

*Be joyful always; pray continuously;
give thanks in all circumstances, for this is
God's will for you in Christ Jesus.*

−1 Thessalonians 5:16

Issue: How do I deal with burnout in the workplace?

A significant issue is eating Mary up inside and ruining her and her family's lives: She's a workaholic, consumed by her job. She wakes up at 4:30 A.M. and is at work by 6:00 A.M. in order to get a good jump on the day. Around 7:30 P.M., she arrives home exhausted. She works almost a full day on Saturday and half a day on Sunday. On Sunday, she and her husband go to church, then she comes home, works for a few hours, and does the weekly chores. On Monday morning, she wakes up and starts the cycle all over again. There is no break; one week slams into the next.

We talked about how Mary could find balance in her life. Mary broke into tears, saying, "I know I should find more balance, but my work demands keep piling up. I can never get caught up." After drying her tears, Mary promised, "Things are going to smooth out in a couple of months. When things get quiet, I'm going to talk to my boss about my schedule." I had already heard this story, several months ago. The demands Mary's employer placed on her were very real. It struck me, however, that she talked as if she had no choice in the matter. I thought, *Who is responsible for this situation?* Is it the company, who placed unfair demands on an excellent employee, or is it the employee, who has accepted the circumstances, even at the expense of her health and her family?

Solution: Keep the important things important.

In today's demanding, fast-paced world, it's easy to lose perspective on what's really important. We need to keep the important things important on a daily basis. Otherwise, we'll fall out of alignment with God's will and risk burnout.

Balancing one's personal and professional life is a serious and complex issue facing many people today. While one chapter of a book won't solve this issue, we will gain insight by learning about two very busy leaders who are enjoying abundant life. We'll learn how their perspective and priorities allowed them to transcend the pressures of work. S. Truett Cathy, Founder and Chairman of Chick-fil-A, a nearly 1,000-unit restaurant chain, followed God's fourth commandment for rest, changing his life and impacting the thousands of employees who work for Chick-fil-A. Bob Naegele, former Chairman and co-owner of Rollerblade, the company that turned in-line skating into an exercise phenomenon, demonstrates how appreciation for God's blessings translated to showing his appreciation to Rollerblade's employees. In both cases, these leaders kept perspective on what was most important and, as a result, enjoyed a harvest of love, peace, and joy.

S. TRUETT CATHY
"Keeping the Important Things Important"

S. Truett Cathy is no stranger to hard work. He also understands the challenges of finding time to rest. Over fifty years ago, Truett and his brother, Ben, opened a small restaurant called The Dwarf Grill in an Atlanta suburb. In 1946, when their first week of business had ended, Ben and Truett sat down, exhausted after the Saturday dinner crowd had all but left. Between the two of them, the brothers had covered six consecutive 24-hour shifts. "What do you think, Truett?" Ben asked. "I think we ought to close tomorrow," Truett replied. From the very beginning, the Cathy brothers told their customers, "We're open 24 hours a day, but not on Sunday."[1]

"Closing on Sunday has become a distinctive principle of my Christian background," says Truett. "From my infancy, my Sunday School teachers and pastors stressed that Sunday is the Lord's Day. I see another reason. God told the Israelites to work only six days so the seventh day could be used for rest. Our bodies and minds need time off to recharge. Lastly, while I was growing up, Sunday was an important day for family times together. For the last 54 years, I've accepted that as a principle and have honored

God by doing it. God has honored us and the business because of it."[2]

The results speak for themselves. On Sunday, you'll find Truett doing the two things he loves most: teaching Sunday School to 13-year-old boys (which he has done for the past 45 years) and being with his family. On the professional front, that single restaurant in 1946 became the cornerstone of Chick-fil-A, now a nearly 1,000-unit restaurant chain.

Truett made the we're not open on Sunday decision in 1946 and has remained committed to the principle ever since. As a result, neither Truett nor any of Chick-fil-A's 40,000 restaurant employees work on Sunday. The traditional business world has called this decision crazy because Chick-fil-A stands to pass on 15 to 20 percent of its sales potential. Truett, Chick-fil-A's Founder and Chairman, sees it in an entirely different way. "I believe God gave His laws not to make life harder, but to make it better," he explains. "This is the formula God has given us for success. In this case it is definitely easier to succeed than to work seven days a week and miss the blessing."

S. Truett Cathy lives his life on a simple principle: Keep the important things in life important. He tells people that success is not defined in only one area of life but in several. "We have to ask ourselves what's really important," he says. "I have seen people who were very successful in business but a total flop in relationships with their family and the other important things in life. I have seen many fathers who loved their children and were anxious to give them the material things they never had as a child, but failed to give them what's really important. For me, the most important thing is my relationship with the Lord and to live my life as a role model for my children. It's nice to have the material things that go with what people generally classify as 'business success'—the nice home and nice cars. All that is secondary when it comes to my family."

I met Truett at Chick-fil-A headquarters in Atlanta during the summer of 1999. I imagined that I was going to meet the very busy Chairman and founder of a fast-food business that grossed almost $800,000,000 in sales in 1998. Instead, the person I met could have been my grandfather. Upon entering the grounds of Chick-fil-A headquarters, I immediately felt a sense of peace and serenity as I drove along a winding road through 73 acres of beautifully landscaped woods and ponds. After parking my car, I walked up to the main entrance and spotted Chick-fil-A's corporate purpose statement. It read:

> To glorify God by being a faithful steward
> of all that is entrusted to us.
> To have a positive influence on all
> who come in contact with Chick-fil-A.

As I entered, I announced my appointment to the receptionist. Quickly, Truett's assistant greeted me with, "I apologize. Mr. Cathy is running about 20 minutes late at lunch with two important visitors. Why not have some lunch in our restaurant while you wait?"

I finally met Truett as he was saying goodbye to his important visitors: two 13-year-old boys who wanted to see Chick-fil-A's operations. In addition to his natural family of 3 children and 12 grandchildren, Truett also has 110 foster children!

After talking with Truett briefly about business and leadership, I saw where his passion truly lies: in his faith in God; his family; the corporate staff; and the 40,000 restaurant employees, the majority of whom are young people whom he considers family. As we finished, Truett gave me a tour of his automobile museum and walked me to the entrance of the headquarters. Summer in Atlanta can be hot, and this day was no exception. As we stood in the parking lot, Truett turned to me and said, "Get in. I'll give you a lift to your car."

"Is this your car?" I asked as we looked at an old, beat-up Toyota pickup. Truett responded, "Nah, I got it for one of my boys who's heading to college. I got it and fixed it up so he could have it to get around. I need to test-drive it to make sure everything is okay."

As we passed the huge bronze plaque with their corporate purpose statement, I reread the first statement: "To glorify God by being a faithful steward of all that is entrusted to us." *Wow, I bet they get some flack for that,* I thought. As if he could hear my thoughts, Truett explained, "Our executive staff initially came up with that statement at a retreat in North Georgia. We were going through tough times back in 1982, and we had an urgency to solve some serious business issues. During a long discussion, my son Dan spoke up. 'Why are we in business?' he asked. 'Why are we here? Why are we alive?' At first, I considered these to be simple questions. 'Why are we wasting time talking about why when we need to talk about how we are going to get past this crisis?' Instead of brushing these questions aside, however, I stopped and said, 'Maybe we do need to answer these questions.'"

Truett went on to explain that they eventually came up with the corporate purpose statement, clear words based on what they believed was most important. In 1983, his staff made a plaque of the corporate purpose statement and gave it to him as a Christmas gift. "I was honored," he recalls. "That statement summarizes my attitude better than anything else. I have always wanted to influence the people in our organization, not by pressing anything on them, but by my attitude, my lifestyle."

As I drove up the interstate to catch a flight back home, I reflected on my visit. I realized that Truett lived up to that corporate purpose statement. He honored God by being a good steward, and he certainly had had a positive influence on me. Despite the business demands and pressures placed on the chairman of a 1,000-unit restaurant chain, this grandpa was living his life with the conviction of what was most important to him.

Understanding Truett's priorities in life clarifies his decision to close all his restaurants on Sunday. Sunday is traditionally the third most active day for restaurant sales, generating approximately 14 percent of the weekly and annual business. Roughly $50 billion dollars will be spent in restaurants on Sundays, and none of it will be spent in a Chick-fil-A. Not only does this translate into lost revenue potential, but it also means Truett has to deal with the considerable pressure that comes from mall developers around the country. They want each of their Chick-fil-As to be open in order to feed their mall's customers.

In his autobiography, *It's Easier to Succeed Than to Fail*, Truett recalls the time he received a letter from a developer whose mall is among the largest in the United States. This letter was received in 1982, a time of increased competition and declining sales. While polite, the letter pressured Truett to open the mall's Chick-fil-A on Sundays. Included were many valid reasons.

The letter closed by explaining: "We have thousands of employees and Sunday strollers who are being denied the right to eat at your place on Sunday afternoon. If you feel that the points we set forth in this letter are valid, and you will consider keeping Chick-fil-A open on Sunday, we would like to offer our contribution in the amount of $5,000 to the churches or organizations of your choice."

Truett responded, explaining in detail his decision. Truett's letter closed with, "Your thoughts are well-received. You are just the kind of person we would like to honor with any reasonable request, but please understand, we cannot compromise on certain principles."[3]

While Truett has had considerable external pressure from the business world, he has never felt any internal pressure to give in. He knows what is important. "You can't be a people pleaser to everyone," he expounds. "Even the people who disagree with you will respect you for your convictions. Besides, how can I teach the 13-year-old boys in my Sunday School class to observe the Lord's day if cash registers are jingling in my restaurants?"[4]

In essence, the principles that drive Truett's personal and professional life take precedence over the pressures of business. Very simply, Truett does not react to business's carrots (rewards) and sticks (business demands). Rather, he responds to the prescription God has laid out for him. This has freed him from the shackles that business demands wanted to place on him.

I came to Truett looking for the answers to the complex issue of work and family balance. What I found was a man who didn't even see it as an issue. He was simply living the life God intended him to live. He keeps the important things important.

ROBERT O. NAEGELE JR.
"Appreciating What's Important"

Meeting with Bob Naegele in his downtown Minneapolis office on a sunny October afternoon, I observed a man having fun. Immediately, I sensed the enthusiasm and joy in his demeanor. I found his enthusiasm odd, considering Bob was waiting to see if his proposal to buy the Minnesota Twins baseball team was going to be accepted. Considering the magnitude of the opportunity, I assumed Bob would be stressed and distracted. That wasn't the case. Bob's circumstances didn't matter; he was enjoying life regardless of them.

It wasn't always that way for Bob. Like most people, he's had his share of challenging times. "My life has been a series of wrecks and rescues," explains Bob. Today, however, Bob Naegele no longer lives in fear; he lives in appreciation. He appreciates what life has given him because he knows it's all a gift from God.

"Fear used to be a big part of my life," Bob says. "I had a deep-seated fear that I was going to come up short. As a child and into adulthood, I feared death. Fear also played a role in my business life. Fear was a motivator. Fear told me to get the job done, or it would cost me my job. Its total motivation is self-preservation. I have had my ups and downs in life, but looking back, every time there was a wreck, there was a rescue."

He is quick to tell of his 1973 personal encounter with Jesus Christ, one that altered the direction of his life, his family's life, and the lives of friends, employees, and business associates. "Through Him, I discovered that God loved me so much that He had sent His son to die for me. I had never known about that love. In addition, I found that God was profoundly interested in me, personally and professionally, and wanted me to succeed in every area of my life. God came to my rescue. On a professional basis, I became a more caring leader. At home, I became a better husband and father. I learned to focus on the important things like trust, respect, and honoring my wife, and they made a huge difference. It was amazing to see the positive impact in our marriage."

Bob's career has spanned close to forty years, half of which was in the outdoor advertising industry. The period between 1985 and 1995 proved to be the most eventful. Bob and 15 others transformed an unknown inline skate into Rollerblade, a company that has created a new way for millions of people to have fun and get exercise.

Bob and his team had their share of challenges at Rollerblade. "My experience at Rollerblade reflected my life: ups and downs and a wreck that needed a rescue," Bob relates. They struggled for years trying to get recognized. Even though they had a great product, no one knew about it. The company was struggling financially and didn't have the resources to market its product the way it needed to be marketed.

Bob recalls, "I remember one particular night when I was growing fearful and anxious about whether we were going to make it. I remember reading Philippians 4:6, 'Do not be anxious about anything, but in everything, by prayer and petition, with thanksgiving, present your requests to God.' I cried out, 'God, please help us . . . nobody knows about Rollerblade.'"

As it turned out, two weeks later, the Minnesota Vikings were playing the Chicago Bears on *Monday Night Football*. During the week of the game, on national television, Mike Ditka, head coach of the Chicago Bears, commented, "We are playing the Vikings at that 'Rollerdome' up in Minneapolis." The rest, as they say, is history. Rollerblade's marketing people jumped on it, and "Rollerblade" became a household word and an overnight success.

The Rollerdome incident helped Bob remember who was really in charge. Today, the incident helps him appreciate how good God has been to him. It also gives him a tremendous appreciation for the others around him who have contributed to Rollerblade's success.

Upon selling his 50 percent share of Rollerblade to Nordica, an Italian ski boot manufacturer, Bob wanted to show his appreciation to Rollerblade's employees. "My father used to say, 'Gratitude unspoken is ingratitude.' So, how do you show gratitude? By saying 'thank you' in a meaningful way."

Rollerblade employee Ann, six months pregnant, called her husband, sobbing. Immediately assuming the worst, his reaction quickly turned to joy as Ann described the note of gratitude and the $11,000 check she received from Bob Naegele and his wife Ellis. Ann was not the only employee to receive a generous gift of thanks from the Naegeles. All 280 employees of Rollerblade received financial gifts, totaling in excess of $4 million. Every employee, from warehouse worker to department manager, received a check based on years of service with the company.[5]

"Ellis and I knew we wanted to do something," says Bob. "We knew our motivation, but we didn't quite know how to go about doing it. We had questions like, 'How do we give the gift?' 'Who should receive the gift?' 'How do we do this fairly?' With our motivation in place, we sought God's guidance on the how and the who. That's the great thing about having a relationship with God. When you are in God's will, things seem to move along. Everything came together smoothly. There wasn't a great deal of guesswork and accountant's projections involved."

The timing of the Rollerblade sale and the details coincided perfectly with the Christmas season. Bob's stock was sold in November 1995, and the details of their gift-giving plan were in place the week before Christmas. "Everything came together at a time that was so meaningful to Ellis and me, a time when you expect the miracles of Christmas to happen. We coordinated with Rollerblade's Vice President of Human Relations what we wanted to do. A list of all the employees was composed, and Ellis and I sat down at our kitchen table and started to write the checks. Waves of joy would overcome us as we saw each person's face in our minds, wrote a note of thanks, and signed the check."

The checks were mailed to employees' homes the week before Christmas. The gift from the Naegeles' hearts began to arrive at employees' homes on December 21. The joy spread rapidly. Rollerblade spokesperson Deborah Autrey said, "It was a complete surprise that came out of the blue. People were laughing and crying, hugging. I have never seen people in such a stupor." When the good news reached Matt, the Director of Product Marketing, he immediately phoned his wife and asked her to open the mail. When she did, Matt heard sobs. He had been with the company 11 years, making his check an estimated $21,120. "It was very moving. It was very heartfelt for us. We were extremely shocked and extremely grateful for his generosity."[6]

As I interviewed Bob, the meaning of the biblical term "cheerful giver" became clear to me. It was evident that joy was a natural part of Bob. During our interview, Bob used the word "joy" 15 times. He repeatedly talked of the waves of joy created by giving. "Joy is infectious; it's explosive; you can't repress it," he explains. "We tried to slip the rock into the pond by being quiet about our gift to the employees. What we found was that giving motivated by God creates a ripple effect that creates significant waves of joy."

The first wave of joy Bob described was when he and Ellis wrote out the checks from their kitchen table. "Ellis and I received our second wave of joy when the thank you letters started to arrive at our home," says Bob. "Letter after letter after letter, it was wonderful! It would happen almost every day for months. One young couple described how they put a down payment on their first house; one couple wrote that they put the money into a fund for their child's education; one guy and his wife sent us a picture of the house they just bought. It was a financial impact, a material impact, but more importantly, it had a spiritual impact."

Here are some of those notes:

"I want to thank you from the bottom of my student loans for remembering even an intern at Rollerblade. I was completely shocked, stunned, and overjoyed all at the same time."

Mindy

"In order to express our heartfelt thanks for your gift, we have made a donation to our church's building fund debt. We have a lot to be thankful for."

Jay and Kathy

"Your gift was incredibly generous and has been placed in our son's name for his education. One day, I will be able to tell Carson about my life with Rollerblade and specifically you and your family. I cannot really explain or describe our appreciation in this card; words don't seem enough. You have touched my life in more ways than you can imagine. I thank you now and one day I would like Carson to thank you in person."

John and Jane

"Your gift has been a source of encouragement. Not only has it been financially uplifting but it has sent a powerful spiritual message. Your gift will never be forgotten. May God bless you always."

Bill and Angela

The third wave of joy came from an unlikely source—the media. Bob's original intent was to keep this gift a private matter, but it didn't take long before the media heard about the generous gifts. Bob recalls receiving a phone call from one of his managers, Matt. "Matt called me and said 'Bob, the press is going to find out. What should we do?' My initial reaction was to keep this story quiet. Then I said, 'Fine, it's a great opportunity to give God the glory.'"

The media did an excellent job communicating a wonderful message. Headlines across the country included "Gifts to Workers Set Naegele Apart," "Gracious Thank

You Bonus Bucks Current Business Trend," and "Sharing the Wealth—A Good Deed Sets a Good Example." As news spread, so did the letters from all over the country. The message of giving touched a wide range of people.

> A teacher wrote, "After teaching for 31 years in Wayzata Public Schools, I have yet to receive more than an apple on American Education Day. I congratulate you for giving part of your profits back to your employees."

> *Larry*

U.S. Senator Byron Dorgan of North Dakota was so moved he decided to make a presentation on the floor of the U.S Senate: "Mr. President, I would like to talk just briefly about two Americans I want to bring to the attention of my colleagues—two heroes of mine. I have never met these men. I talked with one of them on the phone the other day, a fellow named Bob Naegele. I learned about Mr. Naegele and his company in an article I read in the *Minneapolis Star Tribune* when I was traveling though Minneapolis the other day by plane." (He then told the story.) "What this man was saying to them was: You mattered. You people who worked in the plant and factories and helped make this product, you are the ones who made me successful. You made me some money, and I want to share it with you. What a remarkable story. What a hero! It seems to me if more CEOs in this country would understand what Mr. Naegele understands, this country would be a better place."

Joy is a term that can be misunderstood; sometimes made synonymous with happiness or exhilaration. It's so easy to focus on the benevolence of the person, rather than the source of their inspiration. Bob provides insight into the source of his motivation, "I used to be stressed out and fearful, not knowing what my future holds, but now I know Who holds my future."

Bob's definition of joy, one he lives as well as speaks, goes like this: "Joy is an inner feeling provided by God, while exhilaration is the thrill of the moment. That's what business people seek—the thrill of the moment, the thrill of the accomplishment, the landing of the deal. That's why business is so attractive to people. It's also why business people burn out. They are always trying to reach for something more without fully appreciating what they have. But exhilaration is a short-term fix that is driven by circumstance. Joy is much deeper than exhilaration. Joy comes from being motivated by God to do things that matter, that give Him the glory."

CONCLUSION

I was in downtown Minneapolis, racing between appointments. While typically a calm and collected person,

I was in a foul mood on this day. I had just left a frustrating meeting and had 30 minutes to get to my next appointment. The pristine snow-covered streets had turned to April's wet, muddy sidewalks. Watching my shoes get muddier made me more aggravated because I wanted to look good for my next appointment. Knowing that two shoeshine stands were located on the way to my next appointment, I quickly ran to the stand I preferred. It was convenient, provided fast service, and it was directly on my route. There was a wait, so I decided to head to the other shoeshine stand, about a block away.

Thankfully, the second stand had no line. The shoeshine man sat in the big, comfortable chair eating his sandwich. As I raced up to the stand, the elderly man slowly rose to greet me. Neatly dressed in dark blue slacks and a navy shirt, the shirt's emblem proudly displayed his name, Jake. Smiling, he glanced at my muddy shoes and said, "Man, you came to the right place. Hop up and let Jake take care of you."

Jumping into the chair, I began fuming as I recalled the meeting I had just left. I thought about my presentation, given to 10 surgeons from a prestigious medical practice. I had volunteered my services as a consultant/speaker to help teach these physicians the importance of showing respect for their patients. This was a personally significant assignment, as my recent back surgery had been performed by a member of this medical clinic. I felt I had been treated as a spine instead of as a person, and I had hoped to show them how to be more respectful of the patient and how to treat patients as customers.

The meeting was a disaster. The surgeons became indignant, claiming, "We can't afford to do that! Do you know what kind of pressure we are under? For us, time is money. Our caseload is already overloaded. We don't have time to hand-hold every patient."

I had been working long hours under considerable pressure trying to grow my new business. Recalling the details of the meeting set off a chain reaction of negative thoughts: *I get no appreciation for my efforts. I am behind in my work. I probably have to work late to prepare for my presentation tomorrow. I am tired. This day stinks!* I caught myself going through my complaint list and snapped out of it.

I glanced at Jake as he meticulously cleaned my shoes and made sure he had wiped away any trace of mud. I watched as he wrapped an old cloth tightly around two fingers and dipped them into black shoe polish. Using slow circular motions, he rubbed the polish deep into my shoes. I was mesmerized by the meticulous detail he used to shine my shoes. Each stroke began to transform my cold and tired feet into a comfortable and warm respite from the day. I found myself starting to relax.

Without looking up from his meticulous work, Jake said, "Life sure is good, ain't it?" I sarcastically replied, "That depends on your perspective." Jake looked up and said, "I don't know about you, but the good Lord has blessed me with a great 90 years." I asked, "What's the key to your success?" He smiled and said, "Appreciation. I appreciate everything the Lord has given me." Jake went on to describe a life of poverty, struggles, and hard times, yet his stories were filled with many blessings, including a job he loved and a loving family.

His comments stopped me in my tracks. I thought about my meeting with the surgeons. They were upset about their time pressures, and they were clearly not at peace. Financially, they had everything they needed, yet they were stressed and complaining about their circumstances. I thought, *These surgeons have a lot to be thankful for, yet don't appreciate what they have. On the other hand, Jake has lived a tough life, has very little in the way of material possessions, but is truly filled with peace and joy.*

A seven-minute shoeshine transformed a bad day into a good day. My circumstances hadn't changed, but my perspective had. For the first time in my life, I had understood what it meant to be joyful always and to give thanks in all circumstances. Quite frankly, I had never been able to put my arms around the concept of "being joyful always." I thought, *How can I be joyful when I am under such stress and feel so lousy?* It was even more of a stretch when it came to "giving thanks in all circumstances." I believed that it was one thing to muster up some joy, but to actually give thanks in *all* circumstances? Even the bad circumstances? That's a stretch! Jake helped me gain perspective on what's important. He helped me see how God wastes nothing; He uses all circumstances for the good of those who love Him.

Truett, Bob, and Jake help us understand how it is possible to be joyful regardless of circumstances, financial pressure, and time pressure. We all face times when we are overworked and overwhelmed. For many, this is a temporary condition that improves over time. For others, the situation continues, often resulting in burnout and creating a sense of hopelessness. Whether we are just having a bad day or are dealing with a more serious case of hopelessness, don't despair, the answer lies within us. We can rekindle the spirit that lies within us regardless of our present circumstances.

Despite the differences in their backgrounds, Truett, Bob, and Jake had some amazing similarities.

- As Thoreau once said, they hear the beat of "a different drummer." They each lived their lives as an expression of living within the will of God. They didn't define their happiness by the world's standards, but by the will of God. They dictated their pace rather than having the pace dictated for them.
- Although never intending to do so, their decisions made public statements that impacted others. Truett's decision to keep his restaurants closed on Sundays was a statement to his employees regarding the importance of rest and family time. Bob's gifts to the employees of Rollerblade said,

"You matter, and I appreciate what you do." Jake's statement, "I am thankful in all circumstances," has had a significant impact on me and probably many others who needed a shoeshine.

- They each maintained perspective. They kept the important things important and put their circumstances in their proper perspective.
- Each man made a very simple decision in the midst of a complex world. Truett's decision to close his stores could have become complex as he thought through the lost income and strained mall developer relationships, but for him the decision was simple. He was just following God's instructions for success. Bob's decision to reward his employees was fraught with legal and accounting details, yet his desire to show appreciation was heartfelt and simple. He knew the complexities of his decision would work themselves out. Jake could have complained about the things he never had, yet he chose to appreciate and make the best of what he did receive.

Have you ever met someone and felt certain negative or positive vibes from them? Have you ever felt tense when someone else was tense or perhaps felt at ease because someone else was at ease? From these men, I felt love, peace, and joy. These were the by-products of living lives of faith in the midst of a complex world. They each had abundant life and an overflowing spirit. Not only was it evident, but their spirits overflowed to me. I left each meeting feeling energized, loved, and inspired.

When we are burned out, we drain others. Conversely, when we have an overflowing spirit, we inspire and energize others. We simply can't take burnout lightly. Perhaps a simple analogy will help us move in the right direction. Sometimes, we, like a car, have trouble getting going.

Diagnostic Step: Check whether the following symptoms exist:

- My battery needs charging. (I have difficulty getting started in the morning.)
- My idle is set too high. (The pace of my life is too hectic.)
- I left the lights on overnight. (I don't stop thinking about work when I go to bed.)
- I'm riding rough and need a tune up. (I'm not as effective at work as I would like to be.)

Repair Step 1: Charge the battery.

- God is the source of my power and strength. Pray, give thanks, and gain perspective. One simple exercise is to count your blessings (literally). When you're feeling particularly stressed, take a moment and rattle off a list of the things you are thankful for.

Repair Step 2: Set the idle at the right speed.
- Live the pace that's right for you, not the world's pace. Make the important things important and simplify your life by cutting back unnecessary externals.

Repair Step 3: Turn off your lights each night.
- Put closure on each day. Create time to rest daily and weekly and make sure a good night's sleep separates each day.

Repair Step 4: Get a tune up.
- Create a daily rejuvenation plan for the mind, body, and soul. Make sure each day has a morning, afternoon, and evening break.

Repair Step 5: Take a ride in the country.
- Sometimes all we need is a change of scenery. It could be that a small break or vacation will do the trick. Sometimes, we may need to change our environment. If you performed steps 1 through 5, and you still find your energy drained, you may need to find another environment, one that will rejuvenate your soul.

DISCUSSION GUIDE

1. What causes you to burn out from your job? What, specifically, is the root cause?
2. How's your perspective? Are you satisfied or dissatisfied with your present situation? Why?
3. Are your actions in alignment with the things that are most important to you?
4. What changes could you make to keep the important things important?
5. What can you do to rejuvenate your spirit daily?

Notes

1. S. Truett Cathy, *It's Easier to Succeed Than to Fail* (Nashville: Oliver-Nelson Books, 1989), 69.
2. Ibid, 70.
3. Ibid, 75.
4. Ibid, 70.
5. "Rollerblade employees rewarded for service," *Naples Daily News*, January 7, 1996.
6. Ibid.

A Message
of Hope

As we've seen from these each of these 20 leaders, our future is determined by what we believe and do. Every one of our beliefs generates behavior, and every behavior has a consequence. Ultimately, *we become what we believe and do every day.* As we did at the beginning of this book, we can ask ourselves: What are the beliefs that drive our business decisions? Does our faith define who we are at work, or do the business rules define who we are? Are we on the right path?

When you integrate God's principles along with your unique talents, skills, and character, you create a powerful partnership for being successful *in* the world without becoming *of* the world. As a result, your challenges and dilemmas strengthen you to become the successful and significant leader God intended you to be.

What characterizes us as godly leaders? Pressure strengthens us, prioritizing principles over profits enhances our value over time, our character strengthens over time, and, finally, we produce a legacy, in addition to bottom-line results. At the core of our quest for meaningful work is a clash between two masters. In the end, we need to choose.

Walking with God while facing and overcoming life's difficulties is absolutely invaluable to a person—both personally and professionally. Each of the 20 leaders profiled in these pages understood that difficulty is a part of life and that God communicates to us through our circumstances, especially the difficult ones. Each leader also recognized that we can't check God at the door when we go to work.

Our work consumes at least half of our waking life. How can we exclude God from half of our life and be personally and professionally successful? Finally, each leader pursued those things deemed excellent and worthy, regardless of the difficulty faced.

In his valuable book, *My Utmost For His Highest*, Oswald Chambers summarized, "All efforts of worth and excellence are difficult. Difficulty does not make us faint and cave in—it stirs us up to overcome. God does not give us overcoming life—*He gives us life as we overcome*."[1]

The essence of the stories shared in this book is about growing closer to God through our difficulties and dilemmas, one decision at a time. To close, I would like to share the process that defines our success, our purpose for seeking God, and His promises for our reward.

The Process

> *We rejoice in our sufferings, because we know*
> *that suffering produces perseverance;*
> *perseverance, character; and character, hope.*
> *And hope does not disappoint us, because God*
> *has poured out his love into our hearts by the*
> *Holy Spirit, whom he has given us.*
>
> —Romans 5:3–5

The last few years have taken my wife, Sherri, and me on a difficult personal and professional journey. We lost two children through miscarriage, and my business practice suffered in direct proportion to my personal suffering. Monty Sholund, our Bible study teacher, counseled me through every difficult trial and situation.

Consistently, Monty's advice to me was, "Don't miss out on the privilege of your problems." I would share my challenges with him, and inevitably, he would comment, "Oh, this is *sooo* valuable!" Without minimizing my pain, he would share the value of learning and growing closer to God from all circumstances, no matter how difficult.

The 20 leaders who shared their stories with us have each struggled with a difficult dilemma, decision, or situation. They each had the ability to use his or her particular situation or dilemma for his or her growth. In essence, their problems were not stumbling blocks, but stepping stones for personal growth and success. In the same way, the decisions we make in the midst of our dilemmas define us. They shape our character, and they determine our destiny. They are, in short, our journey.

As we struggle, we can choose to focus not on the pain of our present situation, but on the value of the moment. The problems we each face are our own opportunities. Our present situations are part of a much larger process. They are leading us, step by step, to the place God wants us to be.

Our Purpose

O Lord Almighty, blessed is the man who trusts in you.

—Psalm 84:12

Trust in the Lord is a trait common to the 20 leaders. At some point, the leaders took a leap of faith, not knowing what the outcome would be. They each had fears, doubts, and difficulties, yet they each came to a defining moment where they trusted in God more than they trusted in their own understanding of the situation. This moment of faith played a significant role in shaping the destiny of their lives.

In the same way, a time will come when our faith will be tested to the limit—a time when business pressure, intellectual logic, and fear gang up to the point where an easier business decision makes more sense to us than trusting God. This may be the greatest spiritual crisis we will ever face, a point where it is no longer a moral or ethical business decision, but a battle of wills. In fact, choosing God's will may go totally against our business reasoning and may cost us money, a promotion, or even a career. The decision we make is one of our will for our life versus God's will for our life.

At this point, we need to take whatever time is needed to pray for God's guidance. Once we know in our heart what God is calling us to do, we need to trust Him and take that leap of faith. Then He can work.

His Promise

> *No eye has seen, no ear has heard, no mind*
> *has conceived what God has prepared*
> *for those who love Him.*

—1 Corinthians 2:9

We live in a business world that measures success. With every business decision, we calculate a return on investment, a profit margin, or a return on shareholder equity. In doing so, we sell ourselves short. By trying to maximize a return based on what we know, we don't allow ourselves to imagine what can be. God has promised us wonderful things beyond our imagination if only we believe His promises.

Our profiled leaders don't necessarily have a happier life, but they do have a better life. Not only do they live lives filled with personal meaning but they have also made a difference in other people's lives. God does not promise us a happy, carefree life, filled with timely job promotions and lots of amenities. He promises Himself. As Monty Sholund, explains, "God is enough. He is the reward of those who seek Him."

Personally, there would have been no way I would have written this book if I had relied solely on my thoughts and desires. In understanding the time, energy, hassles, pain, problems, and dilemmas that went into the writing process, I would have quickly determined that it wasn't worth the effort. The tangible return on investment simply did not make sense.

However, as I write the last words of this book, I know that I've already been blessed beyond my imagination. I've been blessed by the stories of these remarkable leaders, and I've been blessed by a closer relationship with God. Those dividends are beyond measure.

My prayer is that this book has helped you think about God and His plan for your life. God loves you and wants you to prosper. He has prepared something for you that is beyond comprehension now, but will be revealed to you over time. May God bless you on your journey.

Note

1. Oswald Chambers, as edited by James G. Reimann, *My Utmost for His Highest* (Grand Rapids, MI: Discovery House Publishers, 1992), Devotional July 7.

Further Reading

Beckett, John D., *Loving Monday: Succeeding in Business Without Selling Your Soul*

Buford, Bob, *Halftime: Changing Your Game Plan from Success to Significance*

Cathy, S. Truett, *It's Easier to Succeed Than to Fail*

Colangelo, Jerry, *How You Play the Game*

Melrose, Ken, *Making the Grass Greener on Your Side*

Pollard, C. William, *The Soul of the Firm*

Index

About the Author

Larry Julian's unique talent is bringing diverse people and organizations together to form partnerships with a shared vision and common purpose. As a facilitator, he helps organizations build partnerships that minimize win-lose situations and maximize common gain. As a coach, Larry works one-on-one with leaders to help them work through stressful dilemmas and build better working relationships. He uses his experience consulting with the corporate, government, and community sectors in successful speaking, facilitating, and coaching engagements.

Over the past several years, Larry has facilitated hundreds of strategic planning and teambuilding retreats. He is a popular speaker on the subjects of win-win partnerships, leadership, ethics, and creativity in the marketplace. His clients have included 3M, American Express Financial Advisors, Amoco, AT&T, General Mills, Honeywell, Mayo Clinic, US West, and hundreds of other large and small companies.

Larry is a member of National Speakers Association and is a graduate of Michigan State University School of Business. He lives with his wife, Sherri, and their daughter, Grace, in suburban Minneapolis.

To contact Larry Julian or request information on Larry's speaking, facilitating, coaching, and consulting services, call 1-888-813-8303 or e-mail *larrysjulian@aol.com*.

Visit *godismyceo.com*

FIND MORE ON THIS TOPIC BY VISITING

BusinessTown.com
The Web's big site for growing businesses!

- ☑ **Separate channels on all aspects of starting and running a business**

- ☑ **Lots of info on how to do business online**

- ☑ **1,000+ pages of savvy business advice**

- ☑ **Complete web guide to thousands of useful business sites**

- ☑ **Free e-mail newsletter**

- ☑ **Question and answer forums, and more!**

Accounting
Basic, Credit & Collections, Projections, Purchasing/Cost Control

Advertising
Magazine, Newspaper, Radio, Television, Yellow Pages

Business Opportunities
Ideas for New Businesses, Business for Sale, Franchises

Business Plans
Creating Plans & Business Strategies

Finance
Getting Money, Money Problem Solutions

Letters & Forms
Looking Professional, Sample Letters & Forms

Getting Started
Incorporating, Choosing a Legal Structure

Hiring & Firing
Finding the Right People, Legal Issues

Home Business
Home Business Ideas, Getting Started

Internet
Getting Online, Put Your Catalog on the Web

Legal Issues
Contracts, Copyrights, Patents, Trademarks

Managing a Small Business
Growth, Boosting Profits, Mistakes to Avoid, Competing with the Giants

Managing People
Communications, Compensation, Motivation, Reviews, Problem Employees

Marketing
Direct Mail, Marketing Plans, Strategies, Publicity, Trade Shows

Office Setup
Leasing, Equipment, Supplies

Presentations
Know Your Audience, Good Impression

Sales
Face to Face, Independent Reps, Telemarketing

Selling a Business
Finding Buyers, Setting a Price, Legal Issues

Taxes
Employee, Income, Sales, Property, Use

Time Management
Can You Really Manage Time?

Travel & Maps
Making Business Travel Fun

Valuing a Business
Simple Valuation Guidelines